Teresa's Bible studies are some of the best c _____
a way to teach biblical truth with profoun _____
winsome and relatable way. This resource is _____

KAT ARMSTRONG, author of *No More Holding Back* and *The In-Between Place*

Teresa, my pink-haired theologian, I want to hug you for writing these studies. You have shared practical, personal, and challenging ways to make the Bible come alive. When a smart woman chases after the heart of God, we all win.

TRICIA LOTT WILLIFORD, author of *You Can Do This* and *Just. You. Wait.*

In a noisy world filled with opinion, it can be difficult to cut through the clutter to find the voice of God and His vision for our lives. Plus, let's face it . . . the Bible is both intriguing and, at the same time, intimidating. Teresa does a beautiful job of taking us into God's heart by walking us through His Word. Her guided studies are for any woman who is wrestling with a sense of direction and believing in her worth. By taking us through the Scriptures in a practical, personal, and powerful way, she equips us to own our *now* and step boldly into our *next*.

MARSHAWN EVANS DANIELS, Godfidence Coach, TV personality, reinvention strategist for women, founder of SheProfits.com

With a relatable voice, Teresa makes studying the Bible approachable for women at any stage of faith. The Get Wisdom Bible Studies are a 360-degree look at God's Word with historical contexts, word studies, hands-on application, and commentary for each day's devotion. The studies are timely with varied messages of practicing contentment, trusting God in hard times, and leading the next generation. Teresa is serious about knowing God and how His character changes His people—the reader is not only encouraged to learn but to *live* the truths in these Bible studies.

BAILEY T. HURLEY, author, blogger, and speaker

Get ready for a Bible study that breaks the mold. Self-proclaimed "Bible nerd" Teresa Swanstrom Anderson has a passion for Scripture that is contagious. But don't you dare think this is a nerdy approach to study. Her warm and approachable style feels like a conversation with a wise and humble friend. Along the way, she will challenge you to *pick up your Bible* as she weaves linguistics, history lessons, and personal stories around a passage. I can't wait to recommend this series to women in our church.

GREG HOLDER, lead pastor at The Crossing; author of *The Genius of One* and *Never Settle*

GET WISDOM BIBLE STUDIES

Saying Yes in the Darkness

7 Weeks in the Book of *Psalms*

Teresa Swanstrom Anderson

NavPress

A NavPress resource published in alliance
with Tyndale House Publishers

NavPress is the publishing ministry of The Navigators, an international Christian organization and leader in personal spiritual development. NavPress is committed to helping people grow spiritually and enjoy lives of meaning and hope through personal and group resources that are biblically rooted, culturally relevant, and highly practical.

For more information, visit NavPress.com.

Visit the author online at teresaswanstromanderson.com.

Saying Yes in the Darkness: 7 Weeks in the Book of Psalms

Copyright © 2020 by Teresa Swanstrom Anderson. All rights reserved.

A NavPress resource published in alliance with Tyndale House Publishers

NAVPRESS and the NavPress logo are registered trademarks of NavPress, The Navigators, Colorado Springs, CO. *TYNDALE* is a registered trademark of Tyndale House Publishers. Absence of ® in connection with marks of NavPress or other parties does not indicate an absence of registration of those marks.

The Team: Don Pape, Publisher; Caitlyn Carlson, Acquisitions Editor; Elizabeth Schroll, Copy Editor; Libby Dykstra, Designer and Illustrator

Author photograph by Dionna McCarthy, copyright © 2019. All rights reserved.

Cover and interior illustrations are the property of their respective copyright holders, and all rights are reserved. Cover and interior image by Libby Dykstra © Tyndale House Publishers; glasses © mixov/Depositphotos; book © hristianin/Depositphotos; directional arrow © janjf93/Pixabay.

Author is represented by Jana Burson of The Christopher Ferebee Agency, www.christopherferebee.com.

Unless otherwise indicated, all Scripture quotations are taken from *THE MESSAGE*, copyright © 1993, 2002, 2018 by Eugene H. Peterson. Used by permission of NavPress. All rights reserved. Represented by Tyndale House Publishers. Scripture quotations marked AMP are taken from the Amplified® Bible, copyright © 2015 by The Lockman Foundation. Used by permission. www.Lockman.org. Scripture quotations marked ESV are from The ESV® Bible (The Holy Bible, English Standard Version®), copyright © 2001 by Crossway, a publishing ministry of Good News Publishers. Used by permission. All rights reserved. Scripture quotations marked NIV are taken from the Holy Bible, *New International Version,*® *NIV.*® Copyright © 1973, 1978, 1984, 2011 by Biblica, Inc.® Used by permission. All rights reserved worldwide. Scripture quotations marked NKJV are taken from the New King James Version®. Copyright © 1982 by Thomas Nelson. Used by permission. All rights reserved. Scripture quotations marked NRSV are taken from the New Revised Standard Version Bible, copyright © 1989 National Council of the Churches of Christ in the United States of America. Used by permission. All rights reserved worldwide. Scripture quotations marked TPT are taken from The Passion Translation,® copyright © 2017, 2018 by Passion & Fire Ministries, Inc. Used by permission. All rights reserved. ThePassionTranslation.com. Scripture quotations marked VOICE are taken from The Voice™. Copyright © 2012 by Ecclesia Bible Society. Used by permission. All rights reserved.

Some of the anecdotal illustrations in this book are true to life and are included with the permission of the persons involved. All other illustrations are composites of real situations, and any resemblance to people living or dead is purely coincidental.

For information about special discounts for bulk purchases, please contact Tyndale House Publishers at csresponse@tyndale.com, or call 1-800-323-9400.

ISBN 978-1-64158-002-1

Printed in the United States of America

26	25	24	23	22	21	20
7	6	5	4	3	2	1

For my sweet love.

Benny, thank you for standing with me through every dark and light time, reminding me to keep saying yes to Christ through it all. I love you.

Let's Connect

Take a few moments to be replenished . . .
so that you can pour into others.

 teresaswanstromanderson.com

 @teresa.swanstrom.anderson

 GetWisdomBibleStudies.com

I can't wait to discover all God is doing in your life through David's story. I'd love to see and read all about it! Post using the hashtag #sayingyesinthedarkness on Instagram, Twitter, and/or Facebook so we can encourage one another as we go through this study.

Teresa

Get to know Teresa

Teresa Swanstrom Anderson is a blogger, author, speaker, and Bible study teacher. Teresa grew up in Seattle, but spent her middle school years in Guatemala and has a deep love for people in developing countries. Now living in Denver, Colorado, with her husband and six children, she spends her days wiping off sticky counters, Instagramming, and blogging at teresaswanstromanderson.com. She is the author of *Beautifully Interrupted* and has published several Bible studies on her blog. The Get Wisdom Bible Studies are her first traditionally published studies, taking her passion for studying the Bible and helping women to a broader audience.

Contents

Introduction

Never walk away from Wisdom—she guards your life;
love her—she keeps her eye on you.
Above all and before all, do this: Get Wisdom!
Write this at the top of your list: Get Understanding!
Throw your arms around her—believe me, you won't regret it;
never let her go—she'll make your life glorious.
She'll garland your life with grace,
she'll festoon your days with beauty.

PROVERBS 4:6-9

As a society, we not only like instant gratification—we expect it. We have on-demand movies, Netflix, and Hulu. When our favorite artist releases a new album, we download it onto our phones. If we want a new book, we can get it on our Kindle or listen to it on Audible with a single click. Even two-day shipping seems too slow for us sometimes, doesn't it?

But here's the thing: Growing in our relationship with Christ isn't necessarily quick. There is no instant download to encountering God. We can't pull up into the Starbucks drive-through and leave minutes later with a full grasp of the Bible and what it says about God and means for our lives.

So if you want a bullet-points-only, CliffsNotes experience of the Bible, this study may not be for you. But don't let that freak you out! I get that life is busy, and I promise—we *can* engage deeply with God through His Word in the midst of everything we're doing without being overwhelmed.

If you are a woman whose life isn't perfect, who struggles balancing all aspects of life and wearing all the hats—but you have a genuine desire to grow in your relationship with Jesus in intentional ways that don't require hours a day—then welcome! I'm hopping up onto my chair and throwing confetti around because, my dear friend, you're exactly where you're supposed to be. Together we're going to see the pages of the Bible come alive—and see the God of the Bible become more a part of our everyday experience as a result.

WHY WE STUDY THE BIBLE

The last time Jesus showed Himself to His disciples after His resurrection, mere moments before His ascension, something happened that is crucial for us to remember as we approach the Bible together. Luke 24:44-45 says, "Then he said to them, 'These are my words that I spoke to you while I was still with you—that everything written about me in the law of Moses, the prophets, and the psalms must be fulfilled.' Then he opened their minds to understand the scriptures" (NRSV).

We should be encouraged: Jesus opened their minds to understand that everything written about Him in Scripture must be fulfilled—but I am certain this isn't the only time Jesus has given individuals unique understanding.

He may even give it to you.

But here's the thing: These men had heard Scripture all their lives. They were ordinary working-class men without higher education. Not one of them had gone to school to become a rabbi, and they did not own a scroll or Bible. Yet because Scripture was read every time these men went to worship and biblical stories were retold throughout their lives, this knowledge was deep within the recesses of their minds and hearts. From childhood, these disciples heard God's Word.

We can know something, however, without understanding it. And that's where the disciples were operating from.

Jesus decided to use this moment before His ascension to turn the spigot, and all their previous knowledge, the buildup of years of knowing God's Word, poured out. Except now, with Jesus' hand on that faucet, everything they had learned and heard through the years suddenly made sense to them.

With the help of Jesus, knowledge was finally tied together with comprehension, and the disciples had a major aha moment.

Just like the disciples, we won't have aha moments every time we open the Bible, worship, or pray. We will have days or even weeks when we don't "feel" any big revelations or hear whispered promptings from the Lord.

Do you feel like you're reading the Bible wrong or even wasting your time without having those heartfelt or aha moments? If you're like me, you want those heart moments all the time. That's when we feel especially close to Jesus. But here's the thing . . . it's not about us. Reading the Bible is not about having God give us a warm fuzzy feeling. It's not to show us how to act and react; neither is it about Him speaking to us. Spending time in the Word is about learning who God is. It's about growing in knowledge of the Creator of the universe and our Lord and Savior. Period.

When I realized a few years ago that the Word of God is not about me but about Him, I was rocked. I realized every verse within every page is written with the intent of us learning more about God's character and love.

> *Every story, every illustration, and every law*
> *loops back around to teach us who He is.*

The Bible obviously shares how we should live and who we should be as lovers of the Lord, but it does so in relation to who God is and how He views us. That's why, whether you've loved Christ for five minutes or five decades, I'm just thrilled to be walking through this study of God's Word with you. Together we get to learn more about who He is! As we continue spending time with Him both in the

Word and in prayer, we'll be more prepared to experience Him when He opens our minds like He did for the disciples.

BEFORE WE BEGIN

The Bible

When I was young, I loved collecting. Specifically, I collected bottle caps and napkins. It's okay, you can laugh—it's totally weird. I had boxes of party napkins. I just loved that they were all different, like little pieces of art. Looking back, it kind of makes sense—I love entertaining and setting a pretty table. I still collect those fun napkins so I'm always ready when someone comes over, but I've also begun to collect something else: Bibles.

Why Bibles? Well, the two-hundred-year-old ones passed down from my grandfather are admittedly pieces of art, but I also have shelves of current versions. Still scratching your head as to why I'd have more than one? Well, let me tell you: because different versions say things in different ways.

A great way of understanding Scripture is consulting various translations. Though these Bibles may be worded differently, they don't ultimately differ in meaning and intent, because they all come from the Greek and Hebrew languages the Bible was originally written in.

Some translations are more literal in interpretation than others, however. For example, both *The Message* (MSG) and the The Voice translation (VOICE) capture the tone and essence of the text, while the New Revised Standard Version (NRSV), English Standard Version (ESV), and Amplified Bible (AMP) translations are known to be more literal, emphasizing word-for-word accuracy, literary excellence, and depth of meaning. In other words, versions like *The Message* should be looked at as a reading Bible (almost like a commentary that illuminates the text), rather than as a literal Bible, which is better for deep study.

Don't feel like you need to be a crazy Bible-lady like me, with shelves full of varying translations. The great thing about the internet is you can simply find different versions online. I encourage you to download the Bible Gateway or YouVersion app on your phone or head to their sites on your laptop. Try out a few different versions, and see which ones resonate with you best. If you have a favorite Bible already, google what the Bible you're using is translated for. Is it written for tone and intended meaning? Or is it translated for literal, word-for-word interpretation? Is it a reading Bible or a studying Bible?

In many weeks of this study, we'll explore a reading version of the passage, such as *The Message*, *The Voice*, or *The Passion Translation*, which will help us grasp the thematic picture in more accessible language. As we break apart each passage and dive in deeper, we will use the literal translations, so make sure you have one at the ready. I'll include the text from *The Message*, but in most cases, you will need to reference your own Bible or the Bible app on your phone for the rest. Make sense? Great!

Commentaries and Resources

If we want to be bold women who love God deeply, we must be women of Scripture. We must love the Bible in a way that surpasses others' opinion and research. To become spiritually literate, we must become a student of the Word. Commentaries and books about the Bible are incredibly helpful, but we need to make sure we're not spending more time in books *about* the Bible than in the *actual* Bible.

To be clear, I'm not saying we shouldn't refer to sermons and use commentaries. It would be foolish not to take advantage of the wisdom of others whom we have deep respect for. God has most certainly given the gift of discernment in regard to unraveling the Scripture to unique individuals.

I often study with a commentary or two nearby (in fact, I currently have three opened here on my desk),[1] but through the years, I've learned how important it is to make my own interpretation and have my own thoughts about a Scripture passage (even if it's mostly questions) before considering someone else's thoughts and interpretation. I need to make sure my first Guide is God, rather than humans.

The first thing I'd like us to do is turn to a resource that can help us wrestle with what we're actually reading in the Bible. As we sort through God's Word, we need to be curious about the meanings beyond simply our initial understanding. That's why, in addition to adding the Bible Gateway or YouVersion app onto your phone, I'd also like you to download the Blue Letter Bible (BLB). This is really important because we're going to reference it All. The. Time.

All of these apps I'm recommending are free, but if you want to download only one, choose the BLB because it has Bible translation options in addition to lots of extra resources. We'll be using this app every day in this study because it allows us to easily dig into the languages of the Bible (the Hebrew and Aramaic, the languages in which the Old Testament was written, and Greek, the New Testament's language).

If your eyes are glazing over and you're beginning to rethink wanting to do our study because "Whaaat? Dissecting Greek and Hebrew sounds hard / boring / not for me"—I get it. But this is something you can do! And digging into the Bible on this level is how we learn to study for ourselves and not have a faith that is spoon-fed to us. We want to make sure we are learning God's truth, right? Not just someone else's thoughts!

The BLB will rock your world if you haven't used it before. It totally changed the way I study. I'll show you really quickly how it can do the same for you. First, let's open the app and click on the search icon at the top. Let's look up something random like Psalm 23. (By the way, depending on whether you're in the app or on the website, you may want to choose a different Bible translation that better aligns with the wording we're discussing in the study—the BLB has a few different options.) Read verse 1 and see what questions come to mind.

Hmmm . . . what does it mean, I shall not want? *Like, I'll literally never want for anything if the Lord is my Shepherd?*

Now this is the fun part. We can figure out what these words mean in the original language so we can better comprehend what God wants us to understand! To get there, tap the number by verse 1. On the screen that pops up, tap on *Interlinear* * (we'll be using this function a lot!). On the next screen, scroll down to the phrase or word that you're wanting to dig into—in this case, *I shall not want.* You'll see that in the Hebrew the word is חָסֵר or *chacer.* What does that word mean? Go ahead and click on it to find out.

On the page that pops up, you'll find all sorts of information about this word: how to say it, what part of speech it is, what its synonyms are. My favorite sections on this page are *Strong's Definitions* and the *Gesenius' Hebrew-Chaldee Lexicon.*

Now, let's say that learning more about the word and its meaning didn't clear up our question. We've started to dig in ourselves and not simply accept someone else's explanation of a biblical passage—but since things are still a little unclear, let's head to the commentaries.

Navigate back to Psalm 23 and click on verse 1 again. This time, click on the *Text Commentaries* option. Some of my favorites in the app are by Matthew Henry and C. H. Spurgeon, but look through all of them to find which ones are most helpful to you. For the purposes of our exploration, let's tap on Spurgeon's Psalm 23 commentary. Here's my takeaway from what he wrote: "I shall not want" means I may not possess all that I wish for, but I am given a spirit of contentment. After all, does God not feed the ravens and cause the lilies to grow? I know that His grace will be sufficient for me.

Other places where you can find cross-references, commentaries, and lexicons online are Bible Hub (biblehub.com) and Bible Study Tools (biblestudytools.com). So many discoveries and insights are just a click away! When you start researching word, context, and

---

* On iPhones, this is called *Interlinear/Concordance;* to get to this function on the website, click on *Tools* next to the verse first.

commentaries in your study of the Bible, that is often the beginning of more questions and jumping down bunny trails of more questions and research. But you know what? The point of spending time in the Bible isn't to check off a task and move on with our day. Second Peter 3:18 (ESV) says, "But grow in the grace and knowledge of our Lord and Savior Jesus Christ. To him be the glory both now and to the day of eternity."

Spending time in the Word and with the Lord is about gaining wisdom and knowledge. So if you decide to bounce around even more than I do within these pages and go down bunny trails that I have yet to discover, do it! You can spend fifteen minutes on a passage of Scripture or fifteen days, months, or years. This is all for you and your relationship with Him!

HOW TO USE THIS STUDY

Who + How

There are several ways you can engage in this study. Here are some tips for each context:

1. *Individually*: If you're doing this on your own, that's great! Write in the margins, highlight sections where God seems to want to get your attention, star things, put big question marks in areas you'd like to dig into further. Get this book messy! This study is a conversation between you and the Lord, so freewrite throughout as you really dig into all the beautiful things He wants to chat with you about!

2. *One-on-One*: We grow most in community, so find a friend who would like to do the study with you! Perhaps you'll meet together every week over coffee or lunch. Or maybe you'll meet over the phone or virtually.

3. *In-Person Group*: If you are doing this study in a group setting,

such as a church Bible study or home group, still strive to be 100 percent honest and authentic in your answers. Often, when we're with other women, we're afraid that they might judge our struggles, anger, pain, or even questions we have for or about God. But when we hide our true selves, we won't see the spiritual, emotional, and relational growth that can come out of time with other people who love Jesus. Of course, if the conversation dives into particular sections or questions that you don't feel ready to share publicly, give yourself permission to not answer. But if the group feels safe and supportive, I encourage you to bring all of yourself—including your messiness. And remember—even when you're in a group, make sure to invest in your daily, personal study! Coming to the group time after careful engagement with the Scripture will help everyone flourish.

For more specific directions on how to use this study as a group, head to GetWisdomBibleStudies.com to download the PDF guide. This guide will map out how to use this resource in an eight-week study and how to focus on questions and themes most beneficial for group discussion, as well as how to create and facilitate a healthy group.

4. *Virtual Group*: If you're not plugged into a group in your local context, why not start your own virtual group via Zoom, FaceTime, Skype, or another video-conference website and app? Or perhaps your friends are super busy and spread across the state or country (or world!), so finding an actual day and time to meet proves difficult. If this is the case, you can start your own Facebook group, decide who will facilitate, and start chatting about what you're learning each day or each week. You and your friends can simply post whenever works best for everyone's individual schedules! Sounds fun, right?

Each day of this study can take you only twenty to thirty minutes, but if you'd like to dig deeper, you'll be learning the skills to explore more deeply in the passage of Scripture and the context of the psalm or story. At the end of each day, you'll be prompted into a time of journaling prayer, so you can meet God with your questions and aches that emerge from this journey of saying yes in the darkness.

When + Where

Before starting this study, consider when in your day would best provide some uninterrupted time to dig in. I know finding time can be so difficult in our busy lives, thanks to jobs, kids, and other responsibilities. But we make time for the things that matter—and I promise, time meeting God through His Word is so worth it.

Personally, though I'm certainly not a morning person (hello, coffee), my brain is most attentive in the morning . . . plus, I really love having time with the Lord to center myself before the chaos of the day begins. Through the years, my family notices when I haven't done this for a few days—my joy, patience, and kindness just isn't what it usually is when I'm in the Word at the start of the day!

Simply can't get up any earlier than you currently do? Maybe you work shifts or have little ones not yet sleeping all the way through the night. I get it, and I've been there. I still encourage you to give God the firstfruits of your time, though. Throughout the Bible, we are encouraged to give the first and best to the Lord. And though we may not have a first crop of corn or a perfect lamb to present to Him, we certainly can give Him the first of our time—not the leftovers. Even if rising earlier in the morning feels impossible in this season, you can still offer Him your firstfruits. Pack a bag with your Bible and this study and do it at the beginning of your lunch hour at work, first break between classes, or the first moments of your child's naptime. The laundry, dishes, and showering can wait. Put Him first.

What You'll Need

This study is meant both to guide you through some of the psalms and life of David and to equip you to forge your own path through God's Word so He can make it alive in your everyday life. As you begin your study, here are a few things to keep on hand:

- A Bible in your favorite translation
- Your phone with the Blue Letter Bible app and BibleGateway or YouVersion downloaded
- A pen (you'll find space to write as we explore David's life and psalms together, but also feel free to scribble in the margins as you need to!)
- A smartphone with internet access so you can watch the short videos that introduce each week (you can find those at GetWisdomBibleStudies.com).
- A place without distraction where you can truly dig in!

One Last Thing

A final note to remember as we go through this study: The Bible was written for us, but it's not written *to* us. The Bible is full of stories, poetry, laws, parables, and such, which were written for people who lived in a different culture thousands of years before any of us were born. So each week in this study, we're going to explore some of the behind-the-scenes aspects of Scripture. We're going to figure out the historical and cultural background. We'll try to learn the *why* of it all.

We need to become not just readers of the Word . . . but *studiers* of it. Only then can we understand what God has *for* us in His Word.

SAYING YES IN THE DARKNESS

The book of 1 Samuel might just be my favorite in the Bible. It is chock-full of drama, action, and God's presence. While a lot happens in 1 Samuel, in this study we're going to focus on the parts of the book that align with some of David's psalms. David was a shepherd boy who became king of Israel, and 1 and 2 Samuel show us a lot about his life. David had a lot of victories, but he also walked through profoundly difficult and painful seasons. David wrote a good chunk of the book of Psalms in the midst of such seasons. Through his psalms, we see how he met God in these points in his life—and what we learn is that hardship and even consequences for sin strengthened his faith and dependence on God. During the times in the darkness, David continued saying yes to God, over and over (and over)! There's a lot we can learn from David because none of us are strangers to darkness, are we?

A few days into a recent January, my life fell apart. One of our kids decided he didn't want to be in our family anymore. A few months later, there was death in the family, and then my husband's dad was in the hospital. Mere months after that, I was called as a character witness in a friend's murder trial. He had been placed on death row over a decade prior. Life was hard. Life *is* hard.

We have a choice to walk with God through it all . . . or not. We can say yes through the darkness, or we can let it envelop us so deeply that we feel we cannot get out. Yes, this is a study about David's life and psalms. But it's more than that. We're trying to see the fuller picture. We're looking for the light in it all.

Psalms is celebrated for its passages of praise but it's also known for sections of lament—of learning how to rest in the hard. But I don't want to just rest in my difficulty and pain; I want to keep moving. This study is about that in-between space: walking from the lament *into* the praise. The stepping out through the difficulty, the living in expectation that God will move and we will see light because He *is* the Light.

Let's get to it!

Take joy,

Teresa

When Darkness Sets In

Psalm 59 + 1 Samuel 19

WEEK 1 • *Day 1*

 READ PSALM 59

None of us is exempt from darkness. We face financial struggles, relational heartache, anxiety, fear, loss. Sometimes it feels like the darkness is unending, and we wonder if we'll ever be able to step into the light again.

David's psalms connect deeply with me because they feel so *true*. He's unflinchingly honest about his pain, his anger, his doubt. We call a lot of these psalms *laments* because David shows us how to come before our God, who loves us and can handle our wounds.

David wasn't some perfect person we simply can't identify with. He had his share of missteps and massively poor decision making— but that's what makes him so special. Through his imperfection, through his anguish and anger and pain, he remains someone whom God Himself refers to as "a man after My own heart" (Acts 13:22, VOICE; see also 1 Samuel 13:14). I want to be that kind of person. I hunger for the Lord to consider me a woman after His own heart and a loyal friend.

> God-friendship is for God-worshipers;
> They are the ones he confides in.
> PSALM 25:14

David understood that to become a friend of his heavenly Father, we must spend time with Him (in this case, through worship), just like in any friendship. His friendship with our heavenly Father formed deeply because of quality time, not a one-and-done mentality. He brought the Lord into his everyday life, not simply a portion of time he carved out now and then. Without quality time spent, a relationship cannot grow. Let's become friends of God as we spend time with Him!

In each of the psalms we will study together, there's a backstory—something from the life of David that we can learn about his friendship with God, and about how that relationship helped him say yes and move forward from lament to praise. As you read our first psalm, Psalm 59, I want you to imagine what may be happening in David's life that would motivate him to pen such words. Don't worry if you don't know much about David (yet!)—just put your imagination to work.

1. As you read Psalm 59, circle all of David's cries for help, and underline any language that displays confidence that God will help in his time of trouble.

1-2 My God! Rescue me from my enemies,
    defend me from these mutineers.
Rescue me from their dirty tricks,
    save me from their hit men.
3-4 Desperadoes have ganged up on me,
    they're hiding in ambush for me.
I did nothing to deserve this, GOD,
    crossed no one, wronged no one.
All the same, they're after me,
    determined to get me.
4-5 Wake up and see for yourself! You're GOD,
    GOD-of-Angel-Armies, Israel's God!
Get on the job and take care of these pagans,
    don't be soft on these hard cases.
6-7 They return when the sun goes down,
    They howl like coyotes, ringing the city.
    Then suddenly they're all at the gate,
    Snarling invective, drawn daggers in their teeth.

They think they'll never get caught.
⁸⁻¹⁰ But you, GOD, break out laughing;
    you treat the godless nations like jokes.
Strong God, I'm watching you do it,
    I can always count on you.
God in dependable love shows up on time,
    shows me my enemies in ruin.
¹¹⁻¹³ Don't make quick work of them, GOD,
    lest my people forget.
Bring them down in slow motion,
    take them apart piece by piece.
Let all their mean-mouthed arrogance
    catch up with them,
Catch them out and bring them down
    —every muttered curse
    —every barefaced lie.
Finish them off in fine style!
    Finish them off for good!
Then all the world will see
    that God rules well in Jacob,
    everywhere that God's in charge.
¹⁴⁻¹⁵ They return when the sun goes down,
    They howl like coyotes, ringing the city.
    They scavenge for bones,
    And bite the hand that feeds them.
¹⁶⁻¹⁷ And me? I'm singing your prowess,
    shouting at cockcrow your largesse,
For you've been a safe place for me,
    a good place to hide.
Strong God, I'm watching you do it,
    I can always count on you—
    God, my dependable love.

PSALM 59:1-17

2. The story behind this psalm may be one you've heard, or it may not. Don't flip around in your Bible yet. Based on this passage alone, what can you take from David's situation?

_____

_____

_____

3. When I'm worried about something, I often grasp the worst-case scenario and dwell on what's unfolding in front of me—before remembering that our heavenly Father is bigger than all of it. Do you think that's what David did here? Why or why not?

_____

_____

_____

4. This psalm is divided into several parts. I've heard some say there are two separate sections within this chapter. Do you agree? How do you think these two sections could be divided and summed up?

_____

_____

_____

Look back at your circling and underlining in the passage. While we do see David go back and forth between complaining and praying, praying and complaining, I feel like that's not all it is. In fact, Charles Spurgeon sees this passage broken apart even further.[1] Fill out this chart and let's see if we can discover the bigger picture of what's going on:

5. What is David doing in the following verses?

verses 1-2	
verses 3-4	
verse 5	
verses 6-7	
verses 8-10	
verses 11-13	
verses 14-15	
verses 16-17 [†]	

Isn't that just how we often talk to God when we're worried and in a place of darkness? We pray and then freak out and complain, then toss in a little praise because we know He's bigger than our circumstances . . . but then we freak, hyperventilate, and complain again.

6. Are you ever worried that God will be upset by your prayer because of your tone or emotions? Why or why not?

7. What does David's back-and-forth tell us about God?

---

† In random order, the theme of these answers are: *declares his confidence in God, complains of his circumstances, sings praise to God, lifts his heart in prayer.*

I have some great news for you: God can handle our freak-outs. He can handle our doubts and our depression. Good friends are able to bring their true feelings to each other, right? Since David was indeed a friend of God, he was able to bring all of his feelings to the Lord. God welcomes our emotions, because we're bringing our full and honest selves into relationship with Him. He understands when we come unglued and fall to pieces. He doesn't become angry when we're pouring our heart out to Him through panic, stress, and worry. In fact, it's not a surprise to Him when we behave this way—He *created* us as emotional beings!

Let's wrap up today in quiet time with God, without an agenda. Talk to Him about what you crave to get out of this study, how you relate to David as you read Psalm 59, or various things about your day. Simply let your words flow to our Father in heaven, who loves you deeply.

Amen.

WEEK 1 • *Day 2*

 READ 1 SAMUEL 19

These days, I love studying the Bible. As in, *looove* it. But there were a lot of years after I invited Christ into my life that I didn't spend time in the Word in a consistent way—let alone enjoy doing it.

I think much of my problem was that stories I'd learned in Sunday school, youth group, and Bible studies made the Bible feel disjointed. I didn't understand how things fit together. I had no comprehension of what was going on culturally or what the language actually meant.

But then I went to Capernwray Bible School in England, where I was required to read through the entire Bible before the end of the spring semester. For months, before every afternoon tea, I'd get cozy on my bed and plug away through the Bible—and my relationship with God's Word began to change. As I stared out the window at the rolling green hills dotted with fluffy white sheep, all those disconnected stories began to connect.

I finally understood backstory and context. I began to understand how one thing led to another.

I realized there are no stand-alone stories in Scripture.

At first, reading the Psalms can feel like walking up to a group of friends who are in the middle of a conversation. I often think, *Huh? Why is the psalmist so worried or overjoyed? What's going on in this passage that I don't understand?* Because we're not privy to the beginning of the story, we have no clue what's going on.

My desire to have a fuller understanding of the story behind David's psalms led me to dig in further. I realized that by using the reference notes in the middle or bottom of each page in my Bible,

I'm able to see the bigger picture. I also happened on some incredible information: that some of David's psalms were written from experiences he had in 1 and 2 Samuel.

1. Let's figure out the backstory to Psalm 59 (the passage we studied yesterday). Flip to 1 Samuel 19 in your favorite translation and pen down the essence of this story.

2. What verse(s) in this chapter seems to relate specifically to Psalm 59?

3. How does your version describe the men sent by Saul in 1 Samuel 19:11? How does David describe the men in Psalm 59?

4. Why do you think the group of assailants are described so differently?

First Samuel was written by the prophet Samuel. Perhaps since Samuel wasn't the one actually in the scary situation, or because he knew David wasn't ultimately captured and killed by these men, he wrote it in a less dramatic way.

Still curious about the dichotomy in the description of these men? Good. I am too.

Head to BlueLetterBible.org or the BLB app on your phone and look up 1 Samuel 19:11, select the *Interlinear* tab, and then click on the word *messenger*. We see that in the original Hebrew, the word *messenger* used here is *mal'ak* (מַלְאָךְ, pronounced *mal-ahk*).[‡]

5. In the space below, write the various definitions of *mal'ak*:

_____

_____

_____

_____

We see here that *mal'ak* means "to dispatch as a deputy; a messenger; specifically, of God, i.e. an angel (also a prophet, priest or teacher):—ambassador, angel, king, messenger."[2]

Anyone else think this description is a little strange? Why don't we see a word more like *ratsach* (רָצַח, pronounced *rah-tsakh*),[§] which leans more toward the assassin and murderer type of definition?

6. Why do you think the work *mal'ak* might be used in this passage rather than a word like *ratsach*?

_____

_____

Truth be known, I've looked and looked and no one seems to be talking about this, so I only have my own thoughts to go from. But I'm encouragd by something Charles Spurgeon said:

---

‡ Forget how to use the BLB app? Head back to the Commentaries and Resources section in the introduction for step-by-step directions on using this fun and impactful resource.

§ Pronunciations for Greek, Hebrew, and Aramaic words are included throughout. I encourage you to try saying these words out loud instead of glossing over them.

The commentators are good instructors, but the Author himself is far better.[3]

All throughout my studying, I'm talking to God, asking Him questions and praying. After all, I don't want my Bible study time to feel like homework, unengaged with the Person I'm trying to get to know. This being said, let me share what I think God is telling me about this passage.

Below is this section of 1 Samuel 19 we're talking about. Remember, verse 11 is what connects with our psalm. Circle each time the word *messengers* is used.

[11] Then Saul sent messengers to David's house to watch for him, so that he might kill him in the morning. But Michal, David's wife, told him, "If you do not save your life tonight, tomorrow you will be killed." [12] So Michal let David down through the window, and he fled and escaped. [13] And Michal took the household idol and laid it on the bed, put a pillow of goats' hair at its head, and covered it with clothes. [14] And when Saul sent messengers to take David, she said, "He is sick." [15] Then Saul sent the messengers [again] to see David, saying, "Bring him up to me on his bed [if necessary], so that I may kill him." [16] When the messengers came in, there was the household idol on the bed with a quilt of goats' hair at its head.

1 SAMUEL 19:11-16, AMP

Here's what I'm asking God about the use of this word *mal'ak*. When Saul sent these messengers, did God perhaps sent some of His as well? Maybe the use of this Hebrew word, which typically refers to an angel or someone of authority specifically sent from God, is meant to remind us that these bloodthirsty men were not alone. Perhaps God's *mal'ak* stood right behind or in front of them to ensure that Saul's evil plan would not be carried out.

Whatever the case, David was not unprotected as he faced Saul's wrath. God never leaves us alone in the darkness. He is with us (Joshua 1:9) and for us (Romans 8:31), no matter what we're facing.

> So do not fear, for I am with you;
> do not be dismayed, for I am your God.
> I will strengthen you and help you;
> I will uphold you with my righteous right hand.

ISAIAH 41:10, NIV

 Let's wrap up today by spending some time talking to our heavenly Father, thanking Him for protection in hard situations:

_____

_____

_____

_____

_____

_____

_____

_____

_____

Amen.

WEEK 1 • *Day 3*

READ 1 SAMUEL 18

Today we're going to get a fuller picture of David as he penned Psalm 59. Let's dig in a little more to what was going on in his life during this time and figure out why on earth Saul wanted him dead.

We learn in 1 Samuel 18 that "in everything [David] did he had great success, because the LORD was with him" (18:14, NIV). David did all he was asked and then some. He went from shepherd boy who delivered food to his brothers in battle (1 Samuel 17:17-19) to the hero of it all (1 Samuel 17:32-51). He was taken into the palace (1 Samuel 18:2) and became the king's number one musician (1 Samuel 16:14-23), his most successful warrior (1 Samuel 18:5, 12-16), his son's best friend (1 Samuel 18:1-4), and his daughter's husband (1 Samuel 18:22-27).

David went from zero to hero with one swing of a stone and was forced to run for his life from the king himself, who couldn't control his envy and sought to kill him (1 Samuel 18:28-29).

I heard once that jealousy has two victims, and that is certainly true here.

1. What was Saul jealous about? Why did he want to kill David? (See 1 Samuel 18.)

_____

_____

_____

_____

_____

In 1 Samuel 19:9-10, we see Saul's attempt to pin David to the wall with his spear while David was playing the harp. David barely escaped with his life (and this was not the first time Saul has attempted to kill David!). The next morning, Saul sent men to David's house to try again to kill the young warrior.

Luckily, David had people on his side who believed in him and loved him dearly. Jonathan, King Saul's son, was David's most cherished friend and simply couldn't understand his father's treatment of David. Jonathan was stuck in the middle and yet never wavered in devotion to either man, loving them both. He knew what his father was up to and warned his best friend that trouble was coming. David's wife Michal (also King Saul's child) must have been observant enough to see her father's plans unfolding outside her front door and warned, "If you don't run for your life tonight, tomorrow you'll be killed." Letting David down through a window, the brave Michal saved her husband, allowing him to escape. She had no idea, of course, but the moment she let David down from that window, she lost the man she loved dearly. Eventually her father would remarry her to someone else. It wouldn't be till years later (after David had several more wives) that David would seek to reclaim her. Michal never had children with either husband.

Saul's jealousy ruined a marriage. He forced a young man to run for his life. He turned his greatest warrior into a fugitive who began living in caves.

There's a little more to this story, though—and it has to do with trustworthiness and obedience in our relationship with God.

My husband, Ben, and I were talking to one of our kids about trust one night. Our teenage son wanted responsibility in something and yet was asking that we put boundaries on something else that he knew he couldn't be trusted with. We told him that responsibility and trust go hand in hand: We could either treat him like the young adult that he is, or we could treat him as a child. We wanted to teach him that he couldn't pick and choose where he liked having freedom and responsibility—and where he didn't. It was a package deal.

We discover this same interplay between trust and responsibility in 1 Samuel 15. Go ahead and read that chapter now.

2. Like our son, Saul thought he could pick and choose where he wanted to obey God. In verse 1, what reminder does Samuel give him?

A few chapters back, Saul made some sacrifices to God on his own instead of waiting for Samuel like he had been asked, so the priest no longer trusted him. Perhaps Samuel wanted to remind the king that it was *God* who placed him in this position of leadership. The One True King in heaven was actually in charge.

Samuel goes on to give Saul God's instructions for dealing with the Amalekites (1 Samuel 15:2-3).

3. Does Saul do exactly as he's been asked?

Samuel goes to meet Saul early in the morning and is told that he has gone to another town to set up a monument in his own honor. (Who does that?! C'mon, Saul.) When Samuel reaches the town of Carmel, the king comes out to greet him, saying, "The LORD bless you! I have carried out the LORD's instructions!" (1 Samuel 15:13, NIV).

Saul is so pleased with himself. I love how Samuel responds with dry sarcasm—basically saying, "Oh yeah? Then what's this bleating of sheep in my ears? Why am I hearing lowing of oxen?" (15:14). Saul tries to make excuses and defend himself, but his disobedience is impossible to cover up.

The next two verses we'll look at, 1 Samuel 15:22-23, have long been underlined in my Bible.

4. Read 1 Samuel 15:22-23 in your favorite translation. What's the most important point from this passage?

We absolutely cannot go ahead of God on things. We may not pick and choose where we will obey, where we can be trustworthy and where we simply sweep things under the rug or ignore God's commands. What we need to ponder is this: Does God want our sacrifices and empty traditions that we do simply for show or because we think we're supposed to do it? Where are our hearts?

Doing something for the Lord is actually worth nothing if it's done purely out of habit rather than out of love. What God wants is an obedient and willing heart! God desires for us to listen and respond in accordance with what He's asked. God would far rather you obey than give something up.

5. What have you sacrificed in your life that you think might justify not obeying in another area?

As Samuel tells Saul that God is ripping the kingdom from his hands and giving it to another man who is better than he (1 Samuel 15:28), Saul apologizes for his actions (of course). It's the same today, isn't it? When someone abuses power and gets caught, remorse and regret slither out of their mouths. But it's often empty and solely spoken to regain power, not because they are actually sorry.

This establishes the beginning of the end of Saul's reign . . . and the anointing of the new king.

6. What happens in chapter 16, soon after this conversation between Saul and Samuel?

Exactly, David and Goliath! It's here that young David becomes a household name . . . and King Saul's anxiety begins to simmer.

7. After learning what happened in 1 Samuel 15—and watching
   the arrival of David on the scene in chapter 16—how might
   you explain Saul's treatment of David?

David was not out for Saul's throne. But Saul simply couldn't
wrap his mind around that fact. The young man who brought joy
and support to the king would soon become a source of anger and
resentment. The king's jealousy went unchecked and boiled over to
the point that he simply couldn't rein it in himself.

8. Let's look back at Psalm 59. Does David's freak-out mode make
   more sense now? Describe a time when it felt like evil was stationed outside your door or a jealous someone was trying to
   take you down. How did you respond?

We get all sorts of storied detail in 1 Samuel 18, and Psalm 59
shows us David's inner turmoil as his life was turned upside down.
But Psalm 59 also shows us something extraordinary: Even as David
was running for his life, internally flailing in fear, we see him saying yes and clinging to God. Like David, we can bring our fear and
confusion to God when our world feels like it's being upended—but
let's also have the courage to move toward Him in the midst of it.

Wrap up today by spending some time with the Lord, reflecting on all you learned today and what He may be wanting to teach you through it.

_____

_____

_____

_____

_____

_____

_____

_____

_____

_____

Amen.

WEEK 1 • *Day 4*

 READ PSALM 59

Friends breathe life into my soul, just as I'm sure they do yours. But like any healthy relationship, true friendships sometimes have growing pains. There will be moments when we find ourselves in conflict and need to figure out what to do in the midst of it, right? We need to learn how to grow deeper as friends through difficulty, rather than allowing it to break the closeness.

Recently, a friend and mentor accused me of something that made my heart incredibly heavy. I didn't see it coming and didn't understand how she thought that of me. I literally felt sick all day and went to bed early with a migraine. My thoughts and prayers swirled through the afternoon and evening hours as I went first to God, and then to my husband and dearest friends, placing this person's accusation at their feet for examination.

"Here's the evidence. Look at it. Sift through it; dig deeply," I told them. "Did I do this? *Am* I doing this?"

I was doubled over in anxiety as I asked the Lord and my friends who know me best to share honestly. I wanted to know the truth so I could grow and ask forgiveness if indeed this accusation was true. Because if so, I had some serious heart-searching to do. What I was being accused of is not reflective of the type of person I want to be.

I called my best friend to tearfully vent, and toward the end of our phone conversation, she said something like this:

"You need to stop and seriously ask God to show you the insides of your heart. Lean into it, even if it's hard and yucky. Who are you at the core, really? Ask Him, being honestly willing to hear His response. Take time in silence with the Lord and go through everything in your mind like you're unpacking a suitcase . . . taking items out, one by one. Let Him show you if there is sin here."

Gosh, what wise advice. I just love having friends that are deeper and wiser than I.

I am still completely and totally devastated. And truthfully, I am really embarrassed that someone would think this thing of me. But I don't believe I did what she has said. I did take my heart to God, and I'm okay with what He unearthed in response. (Not that I don't need to grow in areas, of course. We all need to grow, right?)

If I were laying my story next to David's here in Psalm 59, though, I'd tell you quite honestly, I felt that this person was ready to attack. And she did, to some extent.

Let's look again at Psalm 59:3 (TPT):

See how they set an ambush for my life.
They're fierce men ready to launch their attack against me.
O Lord, I'm innocent; protect me!

In this situation with my friend, I was worried she was going to start spreading her thoughts and lies through our mutual friends. I was afraid she was going to post it on social media and disrupt my ministry. I was scared, and, like David, I felt ambushed.

Yes, my situation is tame compared to David's. Thankfully, I don't have mercenaries stationed outside my home just waiting to kill or capture me the moment I walk out my front door. What I do have though, is a situation where I was afraid the lie was going to swirl around and touch many aspects of my community and influence.

Has someone ever spread venom or lies about you, in jealousy or malcontent? How did you handle it? Did you wig out and try to fix things yourself? Or did you drop to your knees and plead that you would feel the Lord's presence as He walked beside you in it? Or, like me, did you do a bit of both?

1. Write about a time when you dealt with some form of attack. How did you respond within the stress and hurt of that circumstance?

2. What were you most afraid would happen in your situation?

In the wake of lies, death follows. Saul thought something incorrect about David (that he was trying to steal the throne), and he tried to kill him. My friend and mentor thought something incorrect about me, and she severed all ties. The death of that friendship breaks my heart.

Today is going to look a bit different from the rest of the week, and there's a reason for that. You see, we're not just here to learn about these stories. Reading God's Word is about more than just story time! We need to allow Him to draw us into the passage and see what He wants us to learn. Our intentional time with the Lord isn't for simply sitting and reading, remaining slightly disengaged—it is to grow in wisdom and knowledge as we also grow in relationship with Him.

Let's read Psalm 59 again. Perhaps you've had a surprising and devastating time with a friend. Perhaps a coworker or family member has hurt you. Maybe you've felt burned or crushed by the church or your community. Maybe the pain is from a while back, or perhaps it's fresh and recent. Whatever it is, I want you to read this passage with fresh eyes, placing your situation within it. You're welcome to flip back to day 1 and read it there, but I'd really love for you to read it from your actual Bible, so you can take notes in your margins as you go.

3. After rereading this passage, rewrite the psalm using your words and situation. Be vulnerable with God as you write it. I get that this would be an easy thing to skip over, for you to leave these lines below blank. But lean into the idea that it's okay to be freaked out and hurt. It's okay to panic and admit to the Lord that you feel scared and ambushed. Do the gritty; get your hands dirty. It's amazing what God can do with vulnerability.

My Own Psalm 59

After writing that, what are you feeling? Is your pain fresh and full of emotion? Are you asking God why you're in the middle of it or why you had to go through it? Are you blaming the Lord for allowing the situation to happen? Are you angry, or are you at peace, knowing that God is the ultimate Protector?

4. What were your emotions as you concluded your psalm?

5. What can you draw from any hurt you may feel? Are you able
   to see God moving through it in spite of it . . . or *because* of it?
   Can you praise Him for walking with you through this pain?
   Are you able to see the love and kindness of others as you've
   lived through it? Or are you feeling lonely and abandoned, like
   He's the only one you have left?

6. We need to make sure our emotions don't go unchecked. Beth
   Moore once said, "Just as fear often leads to jealousy, most
   negative emotions lead to others."[4] How can we ensure our
   emotions don't fly out of control like Saul's did?

7. What was Saul missing?

   _____ the Holy Spirit in his life

   _____ friends/confidants who could speak life and truth into him

   _____ self-control

   _____ a stable family

   _____ a God who loved him

God offers us encouragement, hope, consolation, and direction
when we come to Him in the midst of our struggles. He speaks to

us through His Spirit, equips us with self-control, reminds us of His love, and surrounds us with people who can speak life into our darkness. Unfortunately, Saul rejected God, and as a result, he pushed away all of those things.

To say yes to God, no matter what season or situation we're in, we have to first be honest with Him about the reality of our pain. We've all been hurt and lied to and deceived—and we've all had jealousy coursing through our veins at times too! God isn't dismissive or judgmental of our honest pain. He wants us to bring it to Him so He can help us pursue life and healing.

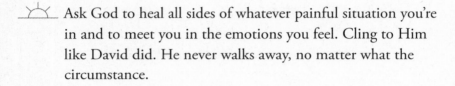 Ask God to heal all sides of whatever painful situation you're in and to meet you in the emotions you feel. Cling to Him like David did. He never walks away, no matter what the circumstance.

Amen.

WEEK 1 • *Day 5*

 READ 1 SAMUEL 18:1-5

Shortly after one of our kids decided he wanted nothing to do with us and left us for six months, we had a death in the family. Mere days later, we received an urgent call saying Ben's dad was in the hospital. It was a hard and devastating season. But something rich and true emerged in the midst of it: God reminded me over and over that *when darkness surrounds, friends step in.* I've said it forever and feel it even more emphatically after going through some seriously hard things these past few years. We have Jesus, yes of course . . . but sometimes the people around us act as His hands and feet.

The story in 1 Samuel 19 and Psalm 59 that we've spent time studying this week surrounds three friends of David: the king (Saul), the king's son (Jonathan), and the king's daughter (Michal). Some of these proved to be loyal friends, but not all.

1. What goes into a friendship that stands the test of time?

The Lord used two of David's friends in a massive wave of protection, and because of their friendship, David was unharmed. But you may be surprised, based on what we've read about Saul so far, that I'm calling him David's friend as well. Let's look at that a little more closely before continuing in our psalm.

In 1 Samuel 16:21 (ESV) we read,

David came to Saul and entered his service. And Saul loved him greatly, and he became his armor-bearer.

Before we continue, I want you to do something quickly. Grab your phone and open the BLB app. Head to the verse just mentioned (1 Samuel 16:21) and click on *Interlinear*, then on the phrase *him; and Saul loved.*

2. What is the Hebrew word used here? _____

Okay, perfect. Remember that word—we'll be coming back to it.

3. Flip to 1 Samuel 18:1, where another of David's friends enters the scene. What do we learn about Jonathan and David's friendship here?

4. We're told that "the soul of Jonathan was knit to the soul of David" (ESV). I always thought the way this was worded seemed a bit strange. Other translations say they became *one in spirit.*[5] They were friends, sure. But why do you think their friendship earned this description?

5. Head over to the BLB and click on 1 Samuel 18:1, then on *Interlinear.* Scroll down to the word *loved.* What Hebrew word is used here?

6. Yay; yes! The same word used about Saul's relationship with David, right? So let's dig into this word. List some of the definitions here:

Let's throw out the sexual aspect of this word because it obviously doesn't fit here. However, "human love for another," love in the aspect of family or friend, and "to have affection for" definitely make sense.[6] Both Saul and Jonathan loved David like family. And yet their friendship with him veered in very different directions. Why was that?

Let's look at 1 Samuel 18:3. We read here that Jonathan and David's friendship included something unique: a covenant. Click on this verse in the BLB. Tap on *Interlinear* and then on *covenant*.

7. What is the Hebrew word for *covenant* here?

8. List some of the words and phrases included in the definition of this word:

9. Where else do we find this word in the Bible? Scroll down to the Concordance in the BLB to see some of the other verses that use this same Hebrew word.

10. Who is the one making the covenant in the majority of these verses?

If we look at David and Jonathan's friendship under the scope of this word *covenant/běriyth*, we see that it's the same one used for pledges between God and humans. A *běriyth* is a treaty, alliance, pledge, or agreement. God made this type of *běriyth* with Abraham (Genesis 15:18), as well as with the nation of Israel through Moses (Exodus 24:7-8; 34:27; Deuteronomy 5:2).

If we dive deeper into the story of David and Jonathan, we learn that under their *běriyth*, Jonathan would be second-in-command in David's future reign (1 Samuel 23:16-18) and David was to protect Jonathan's family (1 Samuel 20:14-16).

The Message writes beautifully about this aspect of their friendship:

> By the time David had finished reporting to Saul, Jonathan was deeply impressed with David—an immediate bond was forged between them. He became totally committed to David. From that point on he would be David's number-one advocate and friend.
>
> 1 SAMUEL 18:1

In 1 Samuel 18:4 (ESV), we see that

> Jonathan stripped himself of the robe that was on him and gave it to David, and his armor, and even his sword and his bow and his belt.

This was a hugely significant gift. By doing this, Jonathan said to David that he recognized the shepherd-turned-soldier as the future king over Israel. The kingship was to have been Jonathan's title. His future. But jealousy did not rear its ugly head in the prince as in the king.

Jonathan walked so closely with God that he knew his father's mistakes cut off the family line to the throne—yet we see no anger. No sadness or attempts to persuade God from the decision He'd already made.

I think about all the times I try to persuade God about what He should do, as if I know better. And as much as I'd like to deny it, sometimes my eyes *do* grow green with envy as I hear about a friend getting something I want, like a book on a bestseller list or their house featured on Anthropologie's feed and website.

Jonathan should have been king. He was a good man who didn't make his father's mistakes or share his envious heart. Yet God's plan for Jonathan's life wouldn't include a crown—but rather friendship with and support for the man who would wear it.

11. Imagine something you want so badly. And then think of your best friend living it instead. What would be your internal and external reponse?

How do you cultivate a heart where you can truly rally around a friend who has everything you thought should be yours—a marriage, a pregnancy, the job of your dreams?

We need to get to the point of trusting Christ enough to embrace the idea that He knows what He's doing. Our plans and dreams may be good, but *His* plan is perfect. Sometimes it doesn't make sense to us, but that doesn't mean it's not right. God does not make mistakes. He's not about to start with your life.

Release your expectations, dreams, and plans to God. Live with open hands, and take a moment to pray for a Jonathan in your life. Not only that, but pray that you *are* a Jonathan to someone. Just as Michal protected David so he could get to safety, you also could be a safe place for friends when they need you the most. Shove all jealousy aside and instead pray that the Lord

would guide you and your friends toward His ultimate desire for
your lives:

Amen.

WEEK 1 *Notes*

Share your biggest takeaways from this week:

Responding in the Darkness

Psalm 56 + 1 Samuel 21

WEEK 2 • *Day 1*

 READ 1 SAMUEL 21

Our daughter Imani is a born actress. She recruits her brothers, sister, and friends to do plays and dance performances, turning the bay windows in our dining room into a stage. Her elaborate pretending astounds me. She's fun, creative, and free in a way I never was when I was her age.

Of course, this flair for the dramatic finds its way into a lot of our interactions. At night, when Ben and I tuck her into the lower bunk, I'll discover that her cheeks are wet with tears. She'll say she's super upset that I hit my head on the bunk (again) or that she doesn't want socks on, or some other goofiness. And just as my heart starts aching for her . . . she bursts out laughing. She gets me every time! (This fake crying stuff is going to be the death of high school boyfriends in about five years.)

I think Imani would love today's Scripture. This week we're going to look at how David chose to respond in a particularly dark season, and he kicks it off with quite the performance. Our response in the darkness—to God and to others—very often boils down to fear or trust. When emotions overwhelm us, it can be hard to turn to God in the midst of it. Will we choose to hold our pain in open hands and trust that God will bring us through—or will our fear cause us to react in ways that we regret?

Fear has a lot of power in our lives. David wrote Psalm 56 from a place of staggering fear—a situation he faced in 1 Samuel 21. Though the entire chapter feels straight out of a Lifetime movie, we'll only be concentrating on verses 10 through 15 this week (don't worry, we'll dig into the rest in the weeks to come).

Before we dive into this week's psalm, I'd like us to become familiar with the corresponding story in 1 Samuel. This passage follows the last chapter we read in 1 Samuel, when Michal convinced David to jump out the window and flee for his life. This week we find out what David did next—and why he made those choices.

1. Read 1 Samuel 21:10-15 and write down the essence of the story (or some of your favorite phrases and portions of this passage).

_____

_____

_____

_____

_____

All sorts of drama in this story, right? My favorite part is where it says David "made marks on the doors of the gate and let his spittle run down his beard" (verse 13, ESV). Or as *The Message* version translates, "he pretended to go crazy, pounding his head on the city gate and foaming at the mouth, spit dripping from his beard."

I mean, whaaat? How desperate and freaked out does a person need to be to behave like this? (I'll just go ahead and answer for you: *very.*)

2. Why is Gath a significant and bold choice for David to flee to? (Hint: Flip over to 1 Samuel 17:4.)

_____

_____

Um . . . what in the world was David doing in enemy territory? I mean, hello . . . this is the land of the Philistines! Don't you think they'd recognize him and be less than thrilled to see the man who killed their champion Goliath—carrying Goliath's sword, no less (1 Samuel 21:8-9)?

3. Once he arrived in Gath and went before the king, what happened that David didn't expect?

It just seems strange, right? David decides to go to the king of Gath—and then is caught off guard when the king not only knows who he is but also what he's famous for. David was likely hoping he could live incognito and hide his true identity—even while holding Goliath's sword in the very land the giant was from. Perhaps David hoped to get a job as a servant, or even went to see Achish with the plan to serve as a mercenary and fight alongside the very men he'd spent years fighting against. Whatever his intent, it was immediately foiled as the king's servants recognized the shepherd-turned-warrior—and David seemed to react immediately out of fear.

Though David definitely thinks creatively and on his feet throughout Scripture, sometimes, like us, he allows fear to overrule him, and he chooses the wrong way. It's possible that in his response to King Achish, he chose to not trust that the Lord was right by his side—and let fear win.

We're going to flip around in our Bibles a bit as we explore fear in more depth. As we do, let's remember that everything in the Bible is related—and since we want to be women of wisdom and knowledge, we need to know how the Bible works together as a whole.

4. Turn to Joshua 1:9. What is your biggest takeaway from this verse?

5. What do you think David should have done when his enemies discovered his identity?

6. How might he have behaved differently if he trusted God a little more and let the Lord be in control of the outcome?

7. Now let's look at another story in Scripture where a God follower fell under the authority of an unfriendly king. Turn to Acts 12:5-17, and share the story in a few sentences below:

King Herod placed Peter (one of Jesus' twelve disciples and a dear friend) in jail. Even in the face of a terrifying situation that could have ended in his death, Peter chose to trust God in the midst of a terrifying situation, rather than let fear and darkness consume him. And God intervened in such a powerful way, didn't He?

We know that God doesn't always rescue us from difficult situations. But we have no way of knowing what would have happened if David had said, "Well, correction, gentlemen—I'm not the king, but yes, I'm the David of which you speak!" Do you think David should have been honest in responding to the king's men, putting trust in a God so big He can perform miracles like He did for Peter?

8. What might have happened if David had been honest?

Scripture doesn't tell us that David took time to pray about what to do when faced with the immediate danger of being recognized. He may have acted out of self-preservation and survival, acting insane as a last-ditch effort to flee. That's the thing about reacting out of fear—we lean so much on our own ability to fix things that we forget we follow a God who is so much more powerful than the thing we fear or the situation we're in. Turning to God in the midst of our fear can be scary, because we don't know how He'll respond. He may not "come through" in the way we want Him to—and so we decide not to turn to Him at all. But only by depending on God can we truly move forward in the darkness. Fear keeps us stuck. Trust is saying yes—to our belief in who God is and whatever He's up to, even if it's not the outcome we're hoping for.

Bring to God a part of your life where you're struggling with
fear. He wants to be with you in it.

Amen.

WEEK 2 • *Day 2*

📖 READ 1 SAMUEL 21

When we find ourselves in a dark season of life, we have a lot of
choices to make. We may feel like we're stuck in the darkness, but
really, we're choosing which direction we want to go by what we say
yes to. Will we say yes to our bitterness? Or will we say yes to God
and the kind of person He's calling us to be?

This choice is particularly difficult because in difficult seasons
we often find ourselves misunderstood and misjudged, and it can be
easier to choose to succumb to that judgment than to stand firm in
our integrity. That's where we find David this week. When he high-
tailed it to Gath, hoping to hide out in the land of Goliath's people,
he likely thought it was the last place Saul would search for him.

Quickly, however, King Achish's guards recognized the shepherd-turned-warrior. I can just see them wide-eyed as they nudged one another, whispering,

> Is not this David the king of the land? Did they not sing to one another of him in dances,
>
> > "Saul has struck down his thousands,
> > and David his ten thousands"?
>
> 1 SAMUEL 21:11, ESV

1. Did you catch the incorrect assessment here? Who did the king's servants think David was?

_____

_____

_____

_____

_____

_____

_____

David's reputation in battle was apparently a topic of conversation even outside the borders of Israel, and the neighboring nations' understanding of who he was had gotten a little out of hand. When I read these verses, I immediately think of the game of Telephone my friends and I used to play when we were little. In fact, it's still my favorite game to play when I'm trying to get cute family photos because there's lots of laughing involved (and what's cuter than a photo of a bunch of kids giggling profusely?). Anyway, as you may remember, things in Telephone get lost in translation pretty quickly—gossip goes from truth to half-truth . . . to not much truth at all. And, in a less fun way, that's something we've all experienced in our lives, isn't it?

2. Share about a time when someone shared something massively incorrect about you . . . or when you wrongly believed something about someone else:

_____

_____

_____

_____

_____

_____

_____

Half-truths or things lost in translation may not always seem all that bad. In this case, the soldiers think David is the king of Israel (foreshadowing, perhaps?). If this is the kind of gossip spreading in the lands surrounding Israel, it's no surprise Saul's jealousy is beginning to run rampant! But that's the thing about half-truths—even when they may seem good, they always cause problems. Choosing to stand against all forms of half-truths and gossip, though, is the path to integrity and a wholehearted, congruent life. As we see in one of David's other psalms, he eventually understood this as well.

3. As you read this passage, circle things you struggle with and underline those you feel you do well:

³ They refuse to slander or insult others;
they'll never listen to gossip or rumors,
nor would they ever harm another with their words.
⁴ They will speak out passionately against evil and evil workers
while commending the faithful ones who follow after the truth.
They make firm commitments and follow through,
even at great cost.
⁵ They never crush others with exploitation or abuse

and they would never be bought with a bribe
against the innocent.
They will never be shaken; they will stand firm forever.

PSALM 15:3-5, TPT

4. I would love the words in Psalm 15 to describe how I act. You too? How can we be women who don't go the drama-gossipy route?

Being known as one who joins into gossip, mistruth, and hearsay makes us untrustworthy and unsafe for people looking for authentic relationship. Psalm 15:3-5 is basically an instruction manual on how *not* to be that girl!

5. Using the text from Psalm 15:3-5, list the instructions for the life of integrity in this Do and Do Not list:

DO	
	•
	•
	•
	•
	•

DO NOT	•
	•
	•
	•
	•

6. What happens if we're able to do these things?

_____

_____

Yes! We'll stand firm forever! Let's head to the BLB and dive into this phrase a little bit more. In Psalm 15:5, click on *Interlinear*, then scroll down to the end of the verse and click on the phrases below, listing their definitions:

7. *He who does* (*'asah*; עָשָׂה, pronounced *ah-sah*):

_____

_____

8. *Be shaken* (*mowt*; מוֹט, pronounced *mote*):

_____

_____

9. Using these definitions, rewrite that last little bit of verse 15:

He (or she) who _____ these things shall
never _____ .

So basically, it takes work to commit to act in this way. We need to be intentional in it. And if we work hard to be a woman of good character (which is basically what the list is helping us do), we will never be moved and fall into gossip, slander, and half-truths.

That's a tall order, isn't it? But one that is so very worth it!

Tomorrow we'll plunge into the actual psalm that corresponds with this chapter in 1 Samuel. As we do, we'll see that while David may have been the victim of gossip, he was also responsible for how he handled himself within it.

 Let's end our time together in prayer. Ask God to reveal the places in your heart and life where you may be slipping into half-truths or gossip, or lay before Him the ways you've been wounded by the gossip of others.

_____

_____

_____

_____

_____

_____

_____

_____

_____

Amen.

WEEK 2 • *Day 3*

READ PSALM 56

My husband and I have six kids: two biological "blondies" and four children from Ethiopia. As you can imagine, life is full and fun and full of laughter . . . but it's also full of healing and trauma and loss.

As I mentioned earlier, my season of darkness that corresponded with writing this study was when one of our children decided he didn't want to be in our family anymore. He'd been with us for several years, but his previous independent life as a street kid made it hard for him to comprehend what a healthy, loving family with rules, boundaries, and expectations looked like. He fought it and fought it until he walked away. Our son's fear of losing control overruled, and he decided to take life on his own shoulders.

His story of moving through that time is his own to tell, but as we explore what it means to say yes in the darkness, I can say that my experience in that season resonates with the pain and fear we see from David in this week's psalm.

1. As you read Psalm 56, underline the parts that stand out to you the most, jotting notes in the margin as to why they do.

1-4 Take my side, God—I'm getting kicked around,
    stomped on every day.
Not a day goes by
    but somebody beats me up;
They make it their duty
    to beat me up.
When I get really afraid
    I come to you in trust.
I'm proud to praise God;
    fearless now, I trust in God.
    What can mere mortals do?
5-6 They don't let up—
    they smear my reputation
    and huddle to plot my collapse.
They gang up,
    sneak together through the alleys
To take me by surprise,
    wait their chance to get me.
7 Pay them back in evil!
    Get angry, God!

Down with these people!
⁸ You've kept track of my every toss and turn
    through the sleepless nights,
Each tear entered in your ledger,
    each ache written in your book.
⁹ If my enemies run away,
    turn tail when I yell at them,
Then I'll know
    that God is on my side.
¹⁰⁻¹¹ I'm proud to praise God,
    proud to praise GOD.
Fearless now, I trust in God;
    what can mere mortals do to me?
¹²⁻¹³ God, you did everything you promised,
    and I'm thanking you with all my heart.
You pulled me from the brink of death,
    my feet from the cliff-edge of doom.
Now I stroll at leisure with God
    in the sunlit fields of life.

PSALM 56:1-13

Gah—I can sure relate to David's psalm! I'll bet you can too. If we read the first section of this psalm in the ESV, we see stark language like "enemy" and "attacker," and that's part of why this psalm hits home for me. In that hard season with my son, Satan was an ever-present assailant and adversary. I did feel trampled, oppressed, and attacked. I was being lied to and lied about, and I was overwhelmingly brokenhearted by it all.

2. Have you ever been in a situation that left you grappling with loss and darkness? What emotions did you wrestle with?

But even when we feel surrounded by enemies, spiritual or otherwise, this psalm points us to a larger truth: We are not forgotten or alone.

3. What does Psalm 56:8 (ESV) say about our tears?

4. What do you think that means? Why would God do such a thing?

God saves our tears because they're important. The honest expression of our pain means something. The Creator of the universe recognizes that we're struggling—and He loves us so much that He doesn't toss our tears away. He keeps them close because He sees their value. He knows they came with a price. And He cares about how we feel, act, and endure.

> You have kept count of my tossings;
>   put my tears in your bottle.
>   Are they not in your book?
> PSALM 56:8 (ESV)

I'm not sure what the word *tossings* means—are you? Let's head to the BLB and find out more about what is going on here. Go to Psalm 56:8, and click on *Interlinear*. Scroll down to find this portion of the verse.

This Interlinear section uses the phrase *of my wanderings*. Huh. Okay, *wanderings* is a little more clear than *tossings*. But let's continue on, jumping further down the bunny trail.

5. Tap on *nowd* (נוֹד, pronounced *node*) and share defining words below:

_____

_____

_____

_____

Well, the definition isn't illuminating much for us, right? Now what? Let's head back, and instead of clicking on *Interlinear*, tap on *Text Commentaries*. Choose your own adventure and decide which commentary you'd like to read. Let's see what theologians have to say about this section of our passage. (Just make sure that as you scroll down, you select one that says Psalm 56.)

6. Write the essence of what the commentary you chose says about verse 8:

_____

_____

_____

These thoughts and insights are from _____

7. How does this explanation help you in the darkness of the struggle you shared above?

_____

_____

_____

_____

Our heavenly Father counts our wanderings. I love that. In fact, whenever I hear the word *wandering*, I immediately think of that famous line from *The Lord of the Rings*: "Not all those who wander are lost."[1] I feel like it applies here perfectly. Though David probably felt lost, the Lord knew he wasn't. "God numbered all the weary steps he took."[2] And He numbers each weary step we take, as well. After my son left, when I thought my devastation would consume me, I needed to remember I was not alone in my pain and grief.

You're not alone in yours, either.

God counts our wandering steps, He keeps our tears in a bottle, and He records it all in His "book of remembrance" (Malachi 3:16, ESV). He writes down all the details, all our circumstances, all our loves and losses. He pens the duration and how they will conclude . . . making notes on the whys and what He'd like us to learn through each experience. He writes it all down because nothing happens without His permission. Yes, even the hard stuff. Because somehow there's strength, hope, and faith to be learned through it. God doesn't *cause* suffering, but He does use our pain to change our perspective. As C. S. Lewis wrote, "Pain insists upon being attended to. God whispers to us in our pleasures, speaks in our conscience, but shouts in our pain: it is His megaphone to rouse a deaf world."[3]

David's time of running from Saul had a purpose, rousing him from a comfortable life and calling him into closer relationship with God. In fact, not long after this time in 1 Samuel, David's trust and friendship with our heavenly Father took a dramatic turn. (We'll talk more about that in the upcoming weeks.) But just remember—those steps you're taking? He's counting them. Those tears? He's saving them. And each moment is being written in His book for a great and meaningful purpose. Find what that purpose is and cling to what He's doing . . . as difficult as it may be in the moment.

 Pray through the remembrance of a time you went through something incredibly hard—but now that you look back, you see that you needed to experience it. Or that the Lord brought something good from it. I'll start it for you . . .

*Lord, it didn't make sense, and there were times
I was angry while wading through
the confusion and grief, but . . .*

Amen.

WEEK 2 • *Day 4*

 READ PSALM 56

The wonderful thing about the Bible is that God can reveal things to us through it that cause us to see His work and His people differently than we might have originally. It's good news for us, because that means God is never doing just one thing in our own stories. He's always at work, unearthing and reshaping and refining.

I found myself pondering this as I went through Psalm 56 again. This whole time, we've been talking about David pretending to be a madman, but what shades of gray do we discover in Psalm 56 that might show us something different about his state of mind?

1. Flip to Psalm 56:4 in your translation and write it here:

So I'm a bit confused here, and maybe you are too. On the surface of the story in 1 Samuel, as explored in the first day this week, it looks like David is reacting purely out of fear. When faced with the threat of something bad happening, he behaves like a crazy person rather than owning up to who he is and trusting God to intervene. But in this verse, David tells us how much he trusts God and won't be afraid, even saying, "What can flesh do to me?" (ESV). Am I missing something?

2. How do you reconcile David's actions and words? Do they correspond or conflict?

David's words in Psalm 56 seem awfully bold for a man seemingly driven to desperation by fear. What if he was actually relying on God to the point that even his seemingly crazy reaction emerged from that relationship? What if God whispered into his ear, "I know this sounds nuts, but I want you to act crazy. Really do it up big, and you will be let go"?

3. Do you think there's any chance God is the one who prompted David to act in this way? Why or why not?

Because we're not told within the pages of Scripture what put this idea in David's head, all we have is speculation. But nothing he did went against anything the Lord has asked of us. David didn't lie; he simply didn't answer. (Check out Luke 23:9 for another example of this!)

Sometimes God asks us to do things that seem crazy. When God asked my husband and me to bring two more children home from Ethiopia—after we had just moved to a new state, and all of our finances were wrapped up in breathing new life into a home deemed "uninhabitable" by the bank—I certainly felt like it was crazy. Where would we find the money to adopt them? He also asked me to start waking up at 4:00 a.m. mere weeks after we became a family of eight because He wanted me to start writing a book.[4] That, too, sounded nuts! Just as nuts as when the Lord asked my parents to move our family to Guatemala in the mid-1990s during a massive time of guerrilla warfare and civil unrest. Sometimes God calls us to things that we don't understand because He sees the whole picture, while we see only a tiny portion.

How we respond when God asks us to do something crazy depends on how much we trust our Lord and Savior. Can we trust Him enough to answer yes when His promptings seem bonkers? David faced the same question, starting when God prompted him— a child! without armor and weapons!—to go up against Goliath, a nine-foot warrior wielding a spear.

4. Share about a time God has asked you (or someone you know) to do something that sounded nutty to the rest of the world:

_____

_____

_____

_____

_____

5. How did you (or the person you know) understand that the prompting came from God?

Let's look at Psalm 56 again. Underline each time David uses the word *trust*, and circle any time he speaks in praise.

¹ Be gracious to me, O God, for man tramples on me;
   all day long an attacker oppresses me;
² my enemies trample on me all day long,
   for many attack me proudly.
³ When I am afraid,
   I put my trust in you.
⁴ In God, whose word I praise,
   in God I trust; I shall not be afraid.
   What can flesh do to me?
⁵ All day long they injure my cause;
   all their thoughts are against me for evil.
⁶ They stir up strife, they lurk;
   they watch my steps,
   as they have waited for my life.

⁷ For their crime will they escape?
   In wrath cast down the peoples, O God!
⁸ You have kept count of my tossings;
   put my tears in your bottle.
   Are they not in your book?
⁹ Then my enemies will turn back
   in the day when I call.
   This I know, that God is for me.
¹⁰ In God, whose word I praise,
   in the LORD, whose word I praise,
¹¹ in God I trust; I shall not be afraid.
   What can man do to me?
¹² I must perform my vows to you, O God;
   I will render thank offerings to you.
¹³ For you have delivered my soul from death,
   yes, my feet from falling,
that I may walk before God
   in the light of life.

PSALM 56:1-13, ESV

Interesting, huh? Despite David's freaked-out reaction when he went to Gath, his reflection in this psalm doesn't sound like he was scared spitless when he was recognized by the guards. I'd always read the story in 1 Samuel as David taking things into his own hands . . . but when we look at the fuller picture, stepping into the Psalms, we get a different perspective. There is no mention of doubt or disbelief that God is in control. Nothing that leans toward an apology, admittance of guilt, or lack of trust and mishandling a situation.

Before we wrap up for the day, let's look at the last section in Psalm 56.

¹⁰ I trust in the Lord. And I praise him!
I trust in the Word of God. And I praise him!

¹¹ What harm could man do to me?
With God on my side I will not be afraid of what comes.
My heart overflows with praise to God and for his promises.
I will always trust in him.
¹² So I'm thanking you with all my heart,
with gratitude for all you've done.
I will do everything I've promised you, Lord.
¹³ For you have saved my soul from death
and my feet from stumbling
so that I can walk before the Lord
bathed in his life-giving light.

PSALM 56:10-13, TPT

This was my yes as I faced the unknown with my son. Through months of ache and emotional torture, sorrow, rejection, and loss threatened to consume, and I begged God for healing and restoration. But in the midst of my cries of pain, I had to step toward Him, clinging to this truth: *And if not, He is still good.* I needed to pray for my son *and* praise the Lord for His goodness. I truly felt Him tell me that He would bring our son home to us, but He didn't give any sort of time frame. I had no idea if that meant a year, a decade, or in heaven. I had to rest in Him in the face of the reality that I might never have my son back with me, close, healthy, and safe. And yet within that recognition, my eyes were opened to these questions:

- How much do I trust our God?
- And doesn't He love my son even more than I do?

Though sometimes I felt more like I was going through the motions, I continued praising and praying, praying and praising— knowing that one day, His life-giving light would not only emit a light glow but also cast out all darkness.

Using Psalm 56 as inspiration, write your own psalm of praise surrounding your hard situation. How can you trust a good God through a painful or seemingly bad season?

_____

_____

_____

_____

_____

_____

_____

_____

Amen.

WEEK 2 • *Day 5*

📖 READ PSALM 56

As I write these words, I'm hunkered down in a cabin in the mountains. Through the windows, I see the sun bouncing brightly off the snow, which came a bit earlier in the year than some people would have liked. I don't mind it, though. It's cozy and simple up here. I've cranked the thermostat up a bit and thrown off my big sweater, and I'm basking in the warmth and my favorite T-shirt, which says, *Love Writes a Beautiful Story.*

I love this T-shirt, not just because it's soft and slouchy. I love it most of all because of the friend who created it. She has seen darkness—the unexpected and painful loss of not only her marriage but also her business and her home. Everything caved in on her, and yet she refused to allow that deep, dense darkness to consume her heart and her future. She was raw and authentic in her struggles and brokenness. She allowed me and other friends in and let us sit with her in it. She had created this T-shirt long before her season of hurt, and yet she still believes the words to be true. Love does write a beautiful story—because God is love and there is no darkness in Him.

David is probably steeped too deeply in survival mode to realize it, but I wonder if at this point he believes that God is actually writing a beautiful story—or any story at all. I wonder if he yet understands that saying yes through these hard times will cause him to grow closer to God and start to see the story He's writing.

1. What story has God written in your life so far? What beauty do you think He might be crafting out of the hard thing you're walking through right now?

After hightailing it away from Gath, David came to the Cave of Adullam (1 Samuel 22:1), which was the perfect place to hide out for a while (we'll explore why next week). David may have been sitting in literal darkness within the walls of the cave, a pit in his stomach, when he first sang the song that became Psalm 56. He didn't have a phone or social media. He couldn't reach out to Jonathan or Michal and ask for their wisdom or their prayers. He was maneuvering through this darkness completely alone.

2. Who do you turn to when things go dark in your life?

David lived hundreds of years before the Holy Spirit would flood the hearts of those who believed in Him (Acts 2). People didn't have the same access to God as we do today, which is why prophets—God's voice to His people—were such a big deal. David was not a prophet, but his relationship with God consisted of more than just meditated prayers and sacrifices. In those days, people knew that God's presence could be found within a tabernacle, but they didn't yet understand that He is everywhere all at once. That's why David's relationship with the Lord was unique—from his early days on the run, we start to see him connecting with God right where he is. Even when David was alone, he was never actually alone.

At the very beginning of the Bible, God created the world and saw that everything He made was good—the light, the earth, the waters, the vegetation, and every living creature (Genesis 1:3-4, 10, 12, 16-18, 21, 25, 31). But then, in Genesis 2:18, for the very first time, God says that something is *not* good.

3. What did God say was not good?

Being alone is not a good thing, and God was the first one to say so. If we follow God, His presence in our lives means that we will literally never be alone (Deuteronomy 31:6). Ever. But just because we're not alone doesn't mean we will never be lonely. After all, we're more connected in today's world than we've ever been, thanks to the internet and social media, and yet loneliness is an epidemic.[5] David, friend of God, wasn't alone in that cave. But as he sat there in the darkness of the cave, processing everything that had just happened, I'll bet he felt profoundly lonely.

Loneliness is painful. But, like many of the painful things we face, it is not wasted. Sometimes, in fact, loneliness is imperative for God's work in our story.

4. What purpose might loneliness have had in this part of David's story?

_____

_____

_____

_____

David had been running without stopping, had already gotten in over his head with an enemy king, and, so far, clearly hadn't stopped to reckon with what was happening or where God might be in it. Now it was just him and God.

5. What might be the purpose of loneliness in your story?

_____

_____

_____

_____

_____

In difficult situations and seasons, God may allow everything else to be stripped away. Loneliness is painful, but it can also be redemptive—it forces us to stop and be quiet, and gives us the opportunity to listen and turn to God. If you're lonely right now, take heart. You're not alone.

Spend some time talking to the One who never leaves you alone. Bring Him your loneliness and ask Him to show you how to lean into Him in the darkness.

Amen.

WEEK 2 *Notes*

Share your biggest takeaways from this week:

Finding God in the Darkness

Psalm 34 + 1 Samuel 21

WEEK 3 ● *Day 1*

 READ PSALM 34

The interesting thing about the psalms of David, particularly as we look at them in light of what was going on in his life as he wrote them, is that he wasn't afraid to bring every kind of emotion before God. Last week, we saw him wrestling with trust in the face of fear, and this week, we're going to look at a psalm he wrote on the other side of that same story in 1 Samuel 21. And we're going to discover more of David's heart as he moves toward God in the midst of a terrifying time. Let's read this week's psalm so we can start digging in:

> ¹ I bless GOD every chance I get;
>   my lungs expand with his praise.
> ² I live and breathe GOD;
>   if things aren't going well, hear this and be happy:
> ³ Join me in spreading the news;
>   together let's get the word out.
> ⁴ GOD met me more than halfway,
>   he freed me from my anxious fears.
> ⁵ Look at him; give him your warmest smile.
>   Never hide your feelings from him.
> ⁶ When I was desperate, I called out,
>   and GOD got me out of a tight spot.
> ⁷ GOD's angel sets up a circle
>   of protection around us while we pray.
> ⁸ Open your mouth and taste, open your eyes and see—
>   how good GOD is.
>   Blessed are you who run to him.
> ⁹ Worship GOD if you want the best;
>   worship opens doors to all his goodness.

¹⁰ Young lions on the prowl get hungry,
  but GOD-seekers are full of God.
¹¹ Come, children, listen closely;
  I'll give you a lesson in GOD worship.
¹² Who out there has a lust for life?
  Can't wait each day to come upon beauty?
¹³ Guard your tongue from profanity,
  and no more lying through your teeth.
¹⁴ Turn your back on sin; do something good.
  Embrace peace—don't let it get away!
¹⁵ GOD keeps an eye on his friends,
  his ears pick up every moan and groan.
¹⁶ GOD won't put up with rebels;
  he'll cull them from the pack.
¹⁷ Is anyone crying for help? GOD is listening,
  ready to rescue you.
¹⁸ If your heart is broken, you'll find GOD right there;
  if you're kicked in the gut, he'll help you catch your breath.
¹⁹ Disciples so often get into trouble;
  still, GOD is there every time.
²⁰ He's your bodyguard, shielding every bone;
  not even a finger gets broken.
²¹ The wicked commit slow suicide;
  they waste their lives hating the good.
²² GOD pays for each slave's freedom;
  no one who runs to him loses out.

PSALM 34:1-22

1. What do you think just happened? Why might David be pouring out so much praise to his heavenly Father?

This praise sounds a lot like it comes from relief, doesn't it? I picture David running off after being released from King Achish's guards, maybe galloping away on a horse as fast as the animal's legs will take him. Once he's a safe distance away from Gath, perhaps he pauses to water his exhausted steed, finds a shady spot nearby to rest and catch his breath, and pens this prayer to his God, who protects him.

2. Reread verse 6, recalling our study from last week. What do you think of this verse?

When David called out, God answered and got him out of a tight spot. (Hmm . . . maybe God really *did* encourage him to pretend he was insane. Who knows?) Personally, I'd like to know more about this verse. Hopefully you do too! My ESV translates it as

> This poor man cried, and the LORD heard him
> and saved him out of all his troubles.

David is obviously referring to himself here when he mentions the poor man, but what does he mean by "poor"? Let's head to the BLB, click on *Interlinear*, and tap on the Hebrew word for *poor*, עָנִי or *'aniy* (pronounced *ah-nee*).

3. What words are listed as definitions?

Okay, that makes sense. I kind of wish they'd just translated that word as *needy*, *weak*, or *afflicted* in the first place. The folks who translate our Bibles don't always use the words that make the most sense to us personally. That's why it's so important to take the time to dive in a little deeper into the Greek (New Testament) and Hebrew (Old Testament). (Otherwise I would have thought maybe David was talking about not having much money in his pocketbook!)

Let's keep going. "The LORD heard him," it says. Sigh. We could spend an entire study on this phrase alone. Sometimes it feels like the Lord doesn't hear us. As if our words fly out into the universe without Him catching them. So let's wrestle with David's assertion here. What does the Bible actually tell us about God hearing us?

If you have a Bible with a concordance (a list of words, themes, and topics, which appears toward the back of the Bible), look there for the word *hears* or *hearing*. You should see several verses spreading from Old to New Testament. If you're using a digital Bible, google *Bible verses about God hearing us* or *what the Bible says about God hearing us*, or something along those lines.

4. Choose one or two verses that you find and write them out:

_____

_____

_____

_____

_____

Do the verses you looked up help you understand what David is saying in Psalm 34? I want to single out a specific verse I came across in my search because the wording both provides some more insight . . . and is a little confusing.

> We know that God does not listen to sinners, but if anyone is a worshiper of God and does his will, God listens to him.
> JOHN 9:31, ESV

5. Why might this verse seem a little strange and confusing?

_____

_____

_____

What exactly is a sinner? According to Dictionary.com, this is the definition:

[**sin**-er] *noun*
a person who sins; transgressor.[1]

Okay, lame. Didn't those dictionary people have a teacher who told them you can't use the word in its definition?

6. Let's research the word *transgress* (verb form of *transgressor*) instead. Look up the definition and write it here:

_____

_____

_____

All right, sure. "To violate a law, command, moral code, etc.; offend; sin."[2] Makes sense. It's essentially what I thought the word meant, and what you probably thought too.

But here's the natural next question: If we're all sinners (and even the best of us still are), does that mean God actually does *not* listen to us and this whole thing is a farce? From time to time, I hear people say that the Bible contradicts itself and therefore cannot be true. This could easily be seen as one of those moments.

But guess what? This verse actually makes perfect sense as we dig into it. The Bible doesn't contradict itself at all here. Things still a little foggy? Let's keep going.

7. Head to the BLB and look up this verse (John 9:31), clicking on *Interlinear*. Tap on the Greek word for sinners, *hamartōlos* (ἁμαρτωλός, pronounced *ha-mar-tō-los*). Now hold on a second, because we're going to scroll down past where we typically land. Continue down to the section that says *Thayer's Greek Lexicon*. Write down the portions written in bold:

Does this make more sense? This verse is talking about someone who is *devoted to sin*, someone who is *not free from sin*. As in, a person who maybe doesn't love Jesus quite yet . . . or isn't ready to live into the freedom He gives. A person who is acting in a way opposite from how we are called to live will not be heard by our heavenly Father because they don't have a relationship with Him.

Hopefully that clears up any confusion with that verse. Remember, God does hear us. And He does care. That's why, in this psalm, David is praising God: because He heard him.

All right, let's head back and look at the second part of Psalm 34:6:

> When I was desperate, I called out,
>   and GOD got me out of a tight spot.

This time when we click on the *Interlinear* and tap on the Hebrew word *heard* (*shama'*; שָׁמַע, pronounced *shah-mah*), we're going to scroll way down again. Like the New Testament has *Thayer's Greek Lexicon*, the Old Testament has the *Gesenius' Hebrew-Chaldee Lexicon*. This time, I'm adding it here to show you the whole entry for this verse:

At first glance, it looks overwhelming, I know. I get it. But don't let your eyes glaze over quite yet. Think of this as sort of a word search.

In a brightly colored pen (so it stands out from all this black text), circle or underline anything that sticks out to you in reference to God hearing us. Then come back when you're done.

. . . Finished? Yay; great!

Okay, so something that stuck out to me right away was the seventh line down when it says "to attend." When I read that, I immediately think that God not only hears but listens in a way that He knows what to do next. He puts my request or whatever I'm praying about into motion.

Further down, under the first "(2)," I see that yes indeed—I was right! "To understand things heard" means having an understanding heart.

And even further, it says "to be regarded, to be cared for . . . to be heard and answered."[3]

That is what we learn from David's words in this psalm: God *does* hear our cries. He listens to every word we utter aloud and to each one whispered in the deepest recesses of our heart. And not only does He do so but He answers them with a yes, no, or wait, putting into motion events and circumstances— even when we don't realize His answer has begun.

שָׁמַע and שֶׁמַע——(1) TO HEAR (Syr., Ch. id., Arab. سمع, Æth. ሰምዐ:), Gen. 18:10; Isa. 6:9; with an acc. of thing, Gen. 3:10; 24:52; Ex. 2:15; and of pers. speaking, Gen. 37:17; 1 Sam. 17:28; followed by 'בְּ and a whole sentence, Gen. 42:2; 2 Sam. 11:26. Specially——(a) *to listen* (anhören, zuhören), *to attend* to any person or thing, followed by an acc. Gen. 23:8, 11, 15; Ecc. 7:5; אֶל 1 Ki. 12:15; Isa. 46:3, 12; לְ Job 31:35; followed by בְּ Job 37:2; but בְּ שָׁמַע is commonly *to hear any thing*, testis auritus fuit (Plaut.), etwas mit anhören, Gen. 27:5; Job 15:8; also, to hear with pleasure, 2 Sam. 19:36; Ps. 92:12.——(b) *to hear* and *answer* (used of God), followed by an acc. Gen. 17:20; Psa. 10:17; 54:4; followed by אֶל Gen. 16:11; 30:22; קוֹל 'בְּ Deu. 33:7; Ps. 5:4; 18:7; 27:7; 28:2; 64:2; Lam. 3:56; בְּקוֹל 'בְּ Gen. 30:6; Deut. 1:45; אֶל קוֹל Gen. 21:17. Sometimes also with לְ of the object, Gen. 17:20.——(c) *to obey, to give heed*, Ex. 24:7; Isa. 1:19; followed by אֶל Gen. 28:7; 39:10; Deut. 18:19; Josh. 1:17; לְ Num. 14:27; בְּקוֹל Gen. 27:13; Exod. 18:19; Deut. 26:14; 2 Sam. 12:18; קוֹל לְ 'בְּ Gen. 3:17; Jud. 2:20; Ps. 58:6.

(2) *to understand things heard*, Gen. 11:7; 42:23. לֵב שֹׁמֵעַ an understanding heart, 1 Ki. 3:9. But אִישׁ שֹׁמֵעַ Prov. 21:28 is, "a man who (truly) heard," a faithful witness, as opp. to a false witness.

NIPHAL——(1) *to be heard*, 1 Sa. 1:13; followed by לְ (*by* any one), Neh. 6:1, 7. *To be heard* is also used for *to be regarded, to be cared for*, Ecc. 9:16; *to be heard and answered*, Dan. 10:12, comp. 2 Ch. 30:27.

(2) *to render obedience, to obey*, Ps. 18:45.

(3) *to be understood*, Ps. 19:4.

PIEL, *to cause to hear, i.e. to call*, i. q. Hiphil No. 3; with an acc. of pers. and לְ of thing to which any one is called. 1 Sam. 15:4, "and Saul called all the people to war." 1 Sa. 23:8.

HIPHIL——(1) *to cause to hear, let hear*, as one's own voice, Jud. 18:25; Cant. 2:14 (to cause to hear acceptably, Isa. 58:4); a cry, Jer. 48:4; with two acc. of pers. and thing, to cause any one to hear any thing, 2 Ki. 7:6; Ps. 143:8; followed by אֶל of pers. Eze. 36:15. Without קוֹל absol. *to utter a voice, a cry*; hence with the addition of בְּקוֹלִי Ps. 26:7; Eze. 27:30 (compare נָתַן בְּקוֹל); specially *to sing*, both with the voice, Neh. 12:42, and to play on instruments, 1 Chr. 15:28; 16:5 (especially with a loud sound, 1 Chr. 15:19, compare נֵצַח). Arab. اسمع a female singer, سماع music.

(2) *to announce, to tell* anything, followed by an acc. of the thing, Isa. 45:21; acc. of pers. Isa. 44:8; 48:5; with two acc. of pers. and thing, Isa. 48:6.

(3) *to call, to summon*, i. q. Piel, 1 Ki. 15:22; Jer. 50:29; 51:27.

Derivatives, שֶׁמַע שֵׁמַע; also, שִׁמְעָה שִׁמְעוֹן, מִשְׁמָע, מַשְׁמַעַת, and pr. n. שִׁמְעָא אֶלְישָׁמָע יִשְׁמָעֵאל יִשְׁמַעְיָה. [See also שְׁמוּאֵל.]

As we wrap up the day, let's go to God in prayer. Share with Him any frustration about feeling like He isn't listening to your petitions and pleas. Or thank Him for His faithfulness, that though you hear nothing but silence, you know He is still by your side, working behind the scenes on your behalf.

_____

_____

_____

_____

_____

_____

_____

_____

_____

_____

Amen.

WEEK 3 • *Day 2*

 READ PSALM 34:1-3

Yesterday we learned that God really does hear us, even in the midst of our hard things. And He will respond to our prayer, even if it's not our first-choice answer. Sometimes He answers in a yes, sometimes it's a no, and often it's simply a wait (which can feel like the most frustrating of all). But there's a deeper question in all of this, beyond whether He hears us or not. Let's head back to the beginning of Psalm 34 to explore a more fundamental question, this time in a translation called *The Voice*.

1. Circle all the instances in Psalm 34:1-3 where David talks about something he will do or wants to do, or an action he's highlighting for us to take part in.

   ¹ I will praise the Eternal in every moment through every
       situation.
     Whenever I speak, my words will always praise Him.
   ² Everything within me wants to pay tribute to Him.
     Whenever the poor and humble hear of His greatness, they
       will celebrate too!
   ³ Come and lift up the Eternal with me;
     let's praise His name together!

Over and over—in fact, six times in these three verses—David is magnifying God's name through action, either telling us what he does or directing us to do something. Is it just me, or is that first line (Psalm 34:1) easier said than done? *I will praise God in every moment and in every situation.*[4] I wrote this part of the study the morning I found out my son emancipated himself from us. And yet, right there in my pain, I read David's words, reminding me to still praise our heavenly Father.

2. Share about a situation when you've had a hard time praising God's name:

_____

_____

_____

_____

_____

_____

_____

I think this sort of praise comes down to something very important:
Do you believe that God is good?

Through your ache and confusion. In your loss and suffering. Despite hardship and struggle. Is . . . God . . . still . . . good?

3. Vulnerably share what you think about God's goodness:

_____

_____

_____

_____

_____

We turn on the television and see news stories about famine and warfare. We hear of boys and girls kidnapped into sex trafficking. Our neighbor shares that their spouse was just diagnosed with terminal cancer, or we learn that thousands are homeless after a recent wildfire. We wonder where God is in it all—and if He *is* good, why do we experience such tragedy? We're not alone in wondering. In his tract *Is God Good?*, Max Lucado says,

> Most, if not all of us, have a contractual agreement with God. The fact that he hasn't signed it doesn't keep us from believing it. I pledge to be a good, decent person, and in return God will . . . save my child . . . heal my spouse . . . protect my job . . . (fill in the blank.) Only fair, right? Yet when God fails to meet our bottom-line expectations, we are left spinning in a tornado of questions. Is he good at all? Is God angry at me? Stumped? Overworked? Is his power limited? His authority restricted? Did the devil outwit him? When life isn't good, what are we to think about God? Where is he in all this?[5]

4. Before we can really answer that big question about God, though, we have to ask a more fundamental one: How do we define *good*?

5. Do you think we all have exactly the same definition? Why or why not?

When we talk about God being good, do we think it means He's nice and kind, never hurting anyone's feelings, helping us feel warm and fuzzy all the time? Do we limit His goodness to the short term? Things are going well right now, therefore He is good?

Or is His goodness bigger than that? Does God work in the long term, even as our short term may feel not-so-good?

As I wade through my own hurt and loss, I sometimes wrestle with God's goodness in my life. And gently, He points me back to other times of hurt and loss I've experienced. I couldn't see it at the time, but on the other side, I've realized something important: Every hard time I've journeyed through, God has strengthened me in some capacity. The "good" I wanted was not what I necessarily got—but He still molded something good within me.

6. Name some ways you can see your situation strengthening you.

_____

_____

_____

_____

But let's not rest on experience alone. What does God's Word show us about His goodness in the darkness?

7. Flip to Daniel 3:8-30 and share the essence of the story below:

_____

_____

_____

This passage tells us about Daniel's friends Shadrach, Meshach, and Abednego. The king was throwing them into a fiery furnace because they would not worship the way they were commanded to. They told the king that *their* King, the One True God, was going to save them from the flames:

> But even if he doesn't, it wouldn't make a bit of difference,
> O king. We still wouldn't serve your gods or worship the
> gold statue you set up.
> DANIEL 3:18

In other words . . . *But if not, He is still good.*

Can you believe their confidence in our heavenly Father? It's astounding. They knew that no matter what happened to them personally, He was still a good and loving God. Circumstances did not change who He was.

Verse 8 in this week's chapter says,

Oh, taste and see that the LORD is good!
　Blessed is the man who takes refuge in him!
PSALM 34:8, ESV

David is being hunted down by a jealous king and lowers himself by pretending to be insane—and yet he, too, sees our God as good.

8. Head to the BLB and look up Psalm 34:8, clicking on *Interlinear* and tapping on this Hebrew word for good: *towb* (טוֹב, pronounced *tobe*). Write down the describing words from either the *Outline of Biblical Usage* portion, *Strong's Definitions*, or the *Gesenius' Hebrew-Chaldee Lexicon* (or all three!).

So God is *beautiful, best, bountiful, fair, gracious, joyful, kind, loving, merry* . . . the list goes on. But how can we learn to believe these things in the midst of our pain? Verse 8 gives us part of the answer. David says, *"Taste and see"* (emphasis added). These two senses encourage movement and involvement. When we taste something, we must stop and place it into our mouths. Not only that, but we must pause long enough to notice the flavor. Have you ever noticed that things always taste different when you see what it is? I think of those blind tasting challenges on TV cooking shows—even experienced chefs can have trouble identifying a taste unless they can see it. We can't actually know the truth of a taste unless we see it—and conversely, seeing alone doesn't help us know what something tastes like.

9. How can the reality of "taste and see" be applied to what David is saying about God's goodness?

_____

_____

_____

_____

Some of my children are athletes, and my husband and I are always spouting the importance of nutrition and how it relates to overall performance. One of our children consistently inhaled donuts, soda, and meals from McDonald's and wondered why his speed and endurance weren't where he wanted them to be. So we asked him to try something: Instead of filling his body with things he'd briefly enjoy, would he allow us to feed him foods that were better for him? We incorporated things into his diet that he wouldn't necessarily choose himself. The first time I brought crispy roasted brussels sprouts to our dinner table, our athlete was less than thrilled and just moved them around on his plate. He saw them and didn't think they were good.

But over time, as he lived into the change of eating "good," he began to understand the fullness of what lay on his plate. He realized that though he may have still chosen a bag of candy over vegetables, the benefit of healthier choices brought a more profound good. It's the same for us. When we choose to truly see something the way Jesus does, it will taste different than we expect.

Pray through what you've learned in our time today, that even if you're in the midst of frustration and doubt, God actually is good and for you:

_____

_____

_____

Amen.

WEEK 3 • *Day 3*

 READ PSALM 34:11

I can be a fearful person. I don't have anxiety per se, but something in the back of my head is always warning me that the other shoe is going to drop. I worry that our middle schooler will go out on a bike ride and be hit by a car, that we'll go to a fair or carnival and our youngest will get kidnapped from the crowd, that when we ride up the chairlift while skiing, one of the little ones will slip beneath the bar and fall, that one of us will get cancer or be in a massive car accident. It's all ridiculous, of course, but fear rises quickly because I care so much about my family. I want them to be healthy, happy, and safe, and anything short of that makes my stomach turn.

The Bible talks a lot about fearing God, but that word means something completely different from the unease I'm talking about.

Today as we continue in Psalm 34, we're going to concentrate on verse 11:

> Come, O children, listen to me;
> I will teach you the fear of the LORD.

ESV

Fear the Lord? We want to teach our children to *fear* Him?

All across the Old and New Testaments, we see passages that refer to fearing God. But what exactly does it mean? Let's flip back toward the beginning of the Bible as we begin studying why this word doesn't mean what we may think it does:

> Moses said to the people, "Do not fear, for God has come to test you, that the fear of him may be before you, that you may not sin."
>
> EXODUS 20:20, ESV

This verse is another great example of why it's important to look into the biblical languages. If we were to read this verse in Exodus as it is written, we'd never know that although *fear* is used twice in this verse, these two words look different in Hebrew (*yare'* and *yir'ah*). Although they're from the same root word, one is a verb and the other is a noun, which gives different nuances and helps us explore different directions. Let's dig into the BLB and learn the different meanings of these words.

1. The first time *fear* is used, it is the verb *yare'* (יָרֵא, pronounced *yah-ray*). As you look through the lexicon in the *Interlinear*, what describing words or phrases jump out at you?

2. The second time *fear* is used, it is the Hebrew noun *yir'ah* (יִרְאָה, pronounced *yir-ah*). Pen down the first definition or translation in the lexicon for this word under (1).

3. If you were to rewrite Exodus 20:20 in your own words, changing both words for *fear* (*yare'* and *yir'ah*) to reflect some of the different meanings you've discovered, how would you rewrite it?

If we hadn't dug into this Scripture the way we did, we might make a serious mistake and think it's saying we should be fearful of a scary God. But no part of Him should fill us with dread or terror. Instead, we should have a healthy respect for Him—a reverence for the One who created the universe and all that is within it.

As we spend time in this study, we'll see over and over how David understood that God deserves extreme admiration and awe. Even after poor decisions and indiscretions, David didn't have to be afraid of God—he knew he could still come to God with a heavy heart and a posture of reverence.

As we seek to understand the whole of the Bible, it's worth fleshing out our understanding of this concept of fearing God a little bit more. What else does the Bible say about fear? The word *fear* is listed over four hundred times in the entire Bible, so we have tons of examples to pull from, but let's flip over to the New Testament this time:

> Why, even the hairs of your head are all numbered. Fear not; you are of more value than many sparrows.
>
> LUKE 12:7, ESV

4. The Greek word used here in Luke 12:7 is *phobeō* (φοβέω). Head to the BLB and look at this word's lexicon. What words or phrases could you use in place of *fear*? Rewrite this verse using the words or phrases that make the most sense to you.

Let's do the same thing with Romans 8:15 (ESV):

For you did not receive the spirit of slavery to fall back into fear, but you have received the Spirit of adoption as sons, by whom we cry, "Abba! Father!"

5. Using words or phrases from the BLB lexicon, how could you rewrite this verse to make more sense to you?

Now that you've gained insight into the different meanings of these words for fear, let's head back to Psalm 34:11. In this verse, where David encourages us to teach our children to fear the Lord, which Hebrew word do you think he used? If you said *yir'ah* (יִרְאָה , pronounced *yir-ah*), then you are 100 percent correct (gold star for you!). David encourages us to have deep respect and reverence for our God and Creator of the universe.

If our God is One we should be afraid of, then how could He be Someone who is full of mercy, grace, and love? He cannot go against His very character. As 1 Corinthians 14:33 reminds us, "God is not a God of confusion but of peace" (ESV). *Peace* translates to *security*, *safety*, and *harmony*. We cannot have a God of fear if He is a God of peace. I'm glad we took the time to figure out what "fear of God" really means, aren't you?

As we wrap up today, ask God how He might want you to come before Him in fear, worship, and deep reverence. How can this posture deepen your relationship with Him?

_____

_____

_____

_____

_____

_____

_____

_____

_____

Amen.

WEEK 3 • *Day 4*

 READ PSALM 34:12-14

A few years back, one of our kids was in a massive bike accident on the way to school. He was transferred from a nearby hospital to the main Children's Hospital campus in Denver. Because I had our youngest kids with me (who were all tiny at the time), I wasn't allowed to ride in the ambulance with him, nor was I allowed in the emergency room with them in tow. Crazy with worry about the extent of his injuries and devastated that our sweet seven-year-old was facing it all alone, I finally entered the sliding glass doors into the hospital after speeding home and dropping the girls off with a friend.

I remember riding up the elevator with two women and a child around the age of ten or so. They were all laughing and teasing one another, and I was incensed. *How can they possibly be so happy? Don't they know where we are? Don't they know that there are children all over this hospital who are sick and dying? How dare they joke around. My first grader is bleeding internally, his liver is lacerated and mangled— and they act like my whole world isn't crashing down around me.*

My internal monologue went from worried to slightly hostile as we continued up, floor by floor. I was so full of grief and heartache that I wanted to tell off these happy people. I was in deep anguish and I was ready to fight. I didn't care with whom.

Sometimes when we're hurting, we want others to feel our pain too. As we know, "hurt people hurt people."⁶ And yet Psalm 34 helps encourage us not to:

> ¹²⁻¹³ Do you want to live a long, good life,
> enjoying the beauty that fills each day?
> Then never speak a lie or allow wicked words
> to come from your mouth.
> ¹⁴ Keep turning your back on every sin,
> and make "peace" your life motto.
> Practice being at peace with everyone.
>
> PSALM 34:12-14, TPT

1. Instead of letting our hurt rule our reactions, what are we to do instead?

2. How can we do that?

Before we get to the key for how to not be ruled by hurt, we need to look a little more closely at Psalm 34:12 (ESV):

> What man is there who desires life
>   and loves many days, that he may see good?

Well, sure, of course David is saying he *loves many days* . . . God just rescued him out of a *tight spot*, remember? If I'd just escaped from my enemies, I'd love that day too. Makes sense that he's in a massively good mood. What can we learn from this even if we're still waiting for that rescue, though?

I just went to the *Interlinear* for this verse in the BLB and discovered a few things. Let's first see what it says under the Hebrew word for *life*, *chay* (חַי, pronounced *khai*).

3. Scroll down through the various sections here in the *Interlinear* section and write down the words that jump out at you in this definition:

_____

_____

_____

_____

Merry, revival, appetite, community, fresh. These are words that would describe someone in a vibrant season of life, yes? Someone with an appetite for fresh growth and vitality! We'll come back to this, but let's keep going for now.

Once again in the BLB, click on the phrase *length of days* in the *Interlinear*. When I think of loving length of days, I think of summertime. The sun sets later, and it's warm enough to sit outside after dinner and watch the kids play, an ice tea or lemonade in hand. But some days are so long, I pray bedtime comes quickly so we can move on to a fresh start in the morning.

4. Looking at the *Strong's Definition* of this *Interlinear* section, write down several words or phrases for *length of days*, the Hebrew word *yowm* (יוֹם, pronounced *yōm*):

For the most part, the words used here easily define *length of day*, right? "The hours between sunrise and sunset," things like that. But I also see the phrase "the warm hours."[7] This brings me right back to that summertime feeling, sitting on the patio after dinner. "The warm hours" makes me think, *Yes! I'll desire life (merriment, and an appetite for fresh growth and vitality) during the comfortable hours. The warm hours where I can sit and bask in its glow.*

But here's the thing: That's not real life. We're not always in a season of warmth where we sit with a cool glass of lemonade in our hands. So how can we still "love many days" during a difficult season?

Verse 13 gives us the answer, telling us, "Keep your tongue from evil and your lips from speaking deceit." But we probably wouldn't label my illogical anger at those people in the elevator as deceit, so let's dig into this word a little deeper. Head to the BLB and click on Psalm 34:13, tapping on the Hebrew word for *deceit* (*mirmah*; מִרְמָה, pronounced *meer-mah*) in the *Interlinear*.

5. What definitions do you see under the *Outline of Biblical Usage* section?

Okay, so it says, "deceit, treachery." Hmm . . . treachery? Surely that doesn't describe what I was feeling in that elevator. Is it?

Let's dig a little deeper. I'd like you to scroll down to the *Gesenius'*

Hebrew-Chaldee Lexicon and look for the word *mirmah*. In fact, I'll make it even easier for you by providing it this time.

מִרְמָה f. (from the root רָמָה Pi. to deceive).—(1) *fraud*, Gen. 27:35; 34:13. אִישׁ מִרְמָה a fraudulent man, Psa. 5:7. אַבְנֵי מִרְמָה fraudulent weights, i. e. made to deceive, Mic. 6:11. מֹאזְנֵי מִרְמָה deceptive scales, Pro. 11:1. Meton. *riches gained by fraud*, Jer. 5:27. Plur. מִרְמוֹת Ps. 10:7; 35:20.

6. Circle the phrase *fraudulent weights*. What do these words indicate to you?

_____

_____

_____

_____

_____

My grief was so unbearable that I was trying to place it on the shoulders of everyone else around me. Sometimes we can be so consumed with our own misery that we can fraudulently put the weight of it onto other people.

7. When have you placed the weight of your own emotions on others, unfairly?

_____

_____

_____

_____

So really, we see that this verse has less to do with the actual act of lying and more about the position of our hearts. As we walk through painful times, it's crucial that we don't heave our hurt onto others because we're miserable. I'm not saying we shouldn't be vulnerable and authentic with our friends and family—we definitely should not bottle things up inside and pretend we're fine. But by the same token, we shouldn't spew venom, thinking it'll make us feel better.

8. Verse 14 says to turn away from evil and do good, and to not only seek peace but pursue it. What's the difference between *seek* and *pursue*? Don't look it up, quite yet. Just write what you think it means in your own words.

_____

_____

_____

_____

_____

_____

Let's head to the BLB one last time today. This time though, I'll provide the *Interlinear* information for you. Underline or circle any words for seek that stand out as significant here:

Strong's Definitions

בָּקַשׁ **bâqash**, [pronounced] baw-kash'; a primitive root; to search out (by any method, specifically in worship or prayer); by implication, to strive after:—ask, beg, beseech, desire, enquire, get, make inquisition, procure, (make) request, require, seek (for).[8]

9. Now underline or circle any words for *pursue* that stand out to you as significant:

Strong's Definitions

רָדַף **râdaph**, [pronounced] raw-daf'; a primitive root; to run after (usually with hostile intent; figuratively [of time] gone by):—chase, put to flight, follow (after, on), hunt, (be under) persecute(-ion, -or), pursue(-r).[9]

10. Replacing *seek* and *pursue* with the synonyms you underlined above, how could you put verse 14 into your own words?

Even if we're sitting in a wintery season or one full of ache and grief, we can strive after peace and chase it, following along as if we're on a hunt for it. Peace isn't something that just happens—it's something we fight for.

This word *peace* (שָׁלוֹם, *shalowm*) also means *completeness, contentment,* and *friendship with God*. But there's so much more to this word than even that. Earlier in our study today when we read out of *The Passion* translation, I noticed a little [a] at the end of verse 14, which corresponds to this footnote text:

The pictographic symbols for the word *shalom* (*shin, lamed, vav, mem*) read "Destroy the authority that binds to chaos." The noun *shalom* is derived from the verbal root *shalam*, which means "to restore," in the sense of replacing or providing what is needed in order to make someone or something whole and complete. So *shalom* is used to describe those of us who have been provided all that is needed to be whole and complete and break off all authority that would attempt to bind us to chaos.

We need to pursue wholeness through our hard situations, even in our pain. We need to chase after our friendship with God, even when things are going opposite of the way we think they should. We need to know that God is with us in the painful winter seasons, just as He is in our summery sit-in-the-backyard ones.

As we wrap up today, I encourage you to write a prayer asking God for tangible ways to search out peace and never give up chasing after it. Where are the places you find yourself bound to chaos? Ask Christ to be your *shalom*, no matter what circumstance and season you find yourself in.

Amen.

WEEK 3 • *Day 5*

 READ PSALM 34:18-22

We could spend an entire week on this last section of Psalm 34! Instead, though, we're going to focus on one key part of it: the courage, fortitude, and depth of obedience through brokenness. We discover a special kind of strength when life becomes difficult. We may feel defeated, shattered, and crushed. But this season we're in is not the end. It is part of our story, though, and we need to decide how we will respond within it.

> ¹⁸ The Lord is close to all whose hearts are crushed by pain,
> and he is always ready to restore the repentant one.
> ¹⁹ Even when bad things happen to the good and godly ones,
> the Lord will save them and not let them be defeated
> by what they face.
> ²⁰ God will be your bodyguard to protect you
> when trouble is near.
> Not one bone will be broken.
> ²¹ But the wicked commit slow suicide.
> For they hate and persecute the lovers of God.
> Make no mistake about it,
> God will hold them guilty and punish them;
> they will pay the penalty!
> ²² But the Lord has paid for the freedom of his servants,
> and he will freely pardon those who love him.
> He will declare them free and innocent
> when they turn to hide themselves in him.
>
> PSALM 34:18-22, TPT

1. Let's begin in verse 18:

The Lord is close to all whose hearts are crushed by pain,
and he is always ready to restore the repentant one.

In the margin of my Bible are a ton of little cross-references (corresponding to those tiny letters within the text of verses). In Psalm 34:18, the cross-references help me discover where else in the Bible something similar is said. Some (like Luke 15:17-24, which is the parable of the Prodigal Son) don't seem to help me much in understanding this verse better. But Psalm 51:17 sure does:

I learned God-worship
    when my pride was shattered.
Heart-shattered lives ready for love
    don't for a moment escape God's notice.

PSALM 51:16-17

Now, when I look up this verse in my ESV, I feel like these verses are translated very differently:

The sacrifices of God are a broken spirit;
    a broken and contrite heart, O God, you will not despise.

2. Why does one version talk about God-worship and one speak of sacrifice? How might they be the same thing?

3. Let's flip back to 1 Samuel 15:22 (ESV, NRSV, and NIV are great translations to look this verse up in). What does Samuel tell King Saul is better than sacrifice?

In the Old Covenant, arguably the biggest way the Jews could worship God was through sacrifice. But sacrifice as an act didn't matter without a heart pursuing God behind the act. God's call to us has always been about love and obedience.

4. Let's look up 1 Samuel 15:22 in the BLB and write down several words or phrases that describe the word *obey* (*shama'*; שָׁמַע, pronounced *shah-mah*).

I love the description "to hear with attention or interest."[10] That certainly sounds like the definition of listening, doesn't it? I'd even go one step further to say that after "hearing with attention and interest," taking action would be the actual act of obedience.

5. How might these words and phrases in 1 Samuel 15:22 and Psalm 51:16-17 help us understand Psalm 34:18 better?

Our sacrifice in the midst of brokenness is obedience to and reliance on God. We hold onto Him white-knuckled, knowing He's all we have to get us through to the other side. As we offer Him that sacrifice, David tells us, He is very near. God is with us. He has not walked away and abandoned us in our desperation and pain.

Not only is God near but also, as David proclaims, He is still working, even when our circumstances scream otherwise. Psalm 34:19 (TPT) goes on to say,

Even when bad things happen to the good and godly ones,
the Lord will save them and not let them be defeated
by what they face.

The ESV says it this way:

Many are the afflictions of the righteous,
    but the Lord delivers him out of them all.

6. Head to the BLB and type in "Psalm 34:19." In the *Interlinear* section, scroll down to the Hebrew word for *delivers* (*natsal*; נָצַל, pronounced *nah-tsal*) and pen down several of the words and terms:

I'm going to be honest: I had a bit of a hard time with this word. I kept thinking about all the people who don't seem to actually be rescued. All the families in the Middle East who live with the terror of bombings and beheadings. All of the people who are sold, kidnapped, or tricked into sex slavery. Where's their rescue, Lord?

But as I continued to pore over these defining words, praying for fresh eyes, the phrase *to be torn out or away* suddenly popped out at me. I felt like the Lord was saying, *Remember, this life isn't it. It's not the end. Sickness and pain do not have the final say. The horrors of earth will not exist in the glories of heaven. I offer each person the breath of eternal life with Me, and even though their rescue may not be here and now, it will be* someday.

David acknowledges that sometimes good and godly people will go through unimaginable pain. He also knows that we will not be defeated and that death is not defeat. In verse 20, we discover something that points toward the ultimate fulfillment of this truth.

> He keeps all his bones;
>> not one of them is broken.
>
> ESV

This verse doesn't mean we will never have a broken arm, leg, or rib. Instead, David's words here are a fantastic example of how everything in the Bible leads us toward the character of God and the death and resurrection of Jesus, our Savior. We are actually reading a prophecy of Jesus here. David may not have even realized it when he wrote these words down. He may have simply been implying that God offers protection.

But here's the thing: There are many places in the Old Testament that point straight to Jesus. If we dig into what David says here in this verse, we are directed to a few places. One is Exodus 12:46, where we read about the Passover Lamb, whose bones are not to be broken when it is sacrificed. And we see this theme again in the New Testament, at Jesus' crucifixion.

7. Flip to John 19:31-37, and write below what it says in verse 36.

Jesus *is* the ultimate Passover Lamb! Pretty amazing, right? The prophet Samuel's reminder to Saul (back in 1 Samuel 15:22) could be seen as foreshadowing Jesus coming as the One True Sacrifice for us all. Because of Jesus' death for our sin, God told the Israelites (and therefore us) that we no longer needed to take part in animal sacrifice. Jesus's own sacrifice (out of His obedience to God) allows us to live out a sacrifice of obedience, no matter what we're facing.

Christ is the Righteous One who was taken out of His suffering in death. But suffering and death didn't have the last word, and they won't have the last word for us either. Verse 21 in this week's psalm speaks about how those who hate the righteous (us) will ultimately be condemned.

Affliction will slay the wicked,
> and those who hate the righteous will be condemned.

ESV

Some of us have been kicked by other people. Perhaps by a spouse, a grown child, a friend we thought we could trust, or a coworker. But as this psalm reminds us, God is the one who wins in the end. And if we are walking with God, then we, too, win! Death cannot keep Him down, and death of a relationship, dream, or desire will not keep us down either. There is always hope, always a future, always love when it comes to Christ Jesus.

Ultimately, that is what Psalm 34:19 says. In the end, all of us who love the Lord will ultimately be "torn away" and delivered . . . because that's what we are: saved. Being saved doesn't mean we're immune to the pain of this world, but it *does* mean that God will deliver us—sometimes we're freed or removed from the circumstance here on earth, but even if we're not, we can look forward to the reality of being forever released from it on the day we find ourselves face-to-face with Him. Sometimes being torn out of a situation looks different than we think it should, but in God's graciousness, He knows the best way to deliver each of us according to what we're going through.

The final verse of Psalm 34 (verse 22) reminds us that we are redeemed and have freedom, though we may be brokenhearted:

The LORD redeems the life of his servants;
> none of those who take refuge in him will be condemned.

ESV

GOD pays for each slave's freedom;
no one who runs to him loses out.

MSG

The LORD redeems the soul of His servants,
And none of those who trust in Him shall be condemned.

NKJV

The Lord has paid for the freedom of his servants,
and he will freely pardon those who love him.
He will declare them free and innocent
when they turn to hide themselves in him.

TPT

8. Using those four translations as a guide, rewrite this verse in a way that helps you remember the freedom you have been given. Look up the words in the Hebrew, if you wish to go one step further:

A final word: Our freedom is not for us alone. As I scrolled down below the lexicon in the BLB entry for Psalm 34:19, I saw that the word *natsal* is used 214 times in 194 verses in the Hebrew concordance. Reading all the verses that use this same word within them, I realized yes, God's hand is at work time and time again to deliver all sorts of people and groups into safety, protection, and freedom. But the thing is—often, it's after He's asked someone else to do something. This is where obedience comes in. His promptings cause action, and we get to assist in His plans of deliverance. Let's not simply wait for Him to pick us up and release us from our current season of pain—let's be women who say yes to His call to action in the darkness.

Take some time in prayer and ask God how He may be asking you to *natsal*, to bring deliverance and to love well amid your pain.

Amen.

WEEK 3 *Notes*

Share your biggest takeaways from this week:

With Others in the Darkness

Psalm 52 + 1 Samuel 21–22

WEEK 4 • *Day 1*

 READ 1 SAMUEL 21–22

As we've worked our way through the first part of 1 Samuel, we've seen that when David was first being chased by King Saul, he was basically in survival mode. He acted first and talked to God about it later. How often do we do the same thing? When we're in crisis mode, sometimes God is the last person we talk to.

1. Reflect on a crisis you've walked through. How did you approach God during that time?

In this week's psalm and story from 1 Samuel, we're going to see David realize that his actions have consequences—and that he needs to consult God's direction first and act second.

To understand the larger context, though, first we need to back up just a smidge. This week's psalm corresponds with events that happened after David's award-winning insanity performance, but it's important to look at some details prior to his flight to Gath. Go ahead and read 1 Samuel 21–22.

Ready? Okay, good.

Because David fled Saul's wrath in such a hurry, he was massively unprepared, setting off without anything more than what he wore on his back. No food, no weapons. Though most of us cannot even imagine the struggle for these immediate needs, it's not as uncommon as we may realize. I have friends who came to the US as refugees, and to them, David's predicament is devastatingly familiar. Another friend fled from an abusive husband, running with her children with nothing more than gas in the car. She, too, can understand some of David's urgency and distress.

David, finding himself without support or supplies, rushed a short two miles to the city of Nob, which was a perfect choice for the fugitive. Why did David beeline to this particular town?

Let's just briefly meet two men, in case they're new to us. Here in 1 Samuel 21:1, we see that David went specifically to see Ahimelech. Who was this guy? He was likely Eli's great-grandson, the grandson of the priest who raised Samuel (1 Samuel 1–3).[1] Samuel, as we know, was the incredible prophet who anointed young David's head with oil, setting him apart as the Lord requested (1 Samuel 16), and prior to that was the one God used to select Saul as king (1 Samuel 9–10). Samuel continued as Saul's spiritual adviser until God withdrew his blessing over Saul's kingship (1 Samuel 15).

So Ahimelech is a man whose family legacy is interwoven with some very important figures in David's life. Ahimelech would "get" what was going on without David having to explain all the behind-the-scenes details. It makes sense, right? In fact, we know this was not the only time David had come to him for prayer and wisdom because the priest tells King Saul in the next chapter,

> Do you think that was the first time I prayed with him for
> God's guidance? Hardly!
>
> 1 SAMUEL 22:15

David is not unlike us. When difficulties come, we run somewhere safe, to someone who "gets us." Right?

This week has been particularly hard with one of my kids. Trauma springs up without warning and blows us over with the intensity of a hurricane. I was wrapping up a phone call with my mother-in-law in the front yard, filling her in and telling her how over my head I felt, when a kind neighbor walked by and cheerfully asked how I was doing. Did I blurt out all the junk we'd been wading through this week? No. I simply smiled, waved, and said I was "doing well!" I was too emotionally exhausted to explain it all to her.

But the next morning, I was able to chat with two of my best friends, who are also going through extremely hard situations. They "get" trauma because they have lived it. I don't need to spell out PTSD and how our child can't think rationally when triggered . . . because these women have walked similar roads.

2. If something devastating happened and you needed a safe or supportive place to go (emotionally, physically, spiritually, whatever the need may be), where or to whom would you run? Why?

There was one little hiccup in David's plan. Ahimelech's brother Ahijah was the man who took over as King Saul's spiritual adviser after Samuel stepped down. In other words, Ahimelech's brother was priest to the very king he was running from! David was probably unsure where Ahimelech's allegiance lay.

3. Instead of stopping to pray, asking for God's protection or guidance in the situation, what did David do instead?

David completely and totally fabricated a story because he was scared. We all know he's not the only one who has ever done this!

4. Share about a time when you lied because you were afraid of what might happen if you told the truth:

5. What is your reaction to David deceiving Ahimelech the priest? Would you do the same to keep yourself safe? If not, what would you do instead?

Matthew Henry's Commentary says this about the interaction:

He [David] told Ahimelech a gross untruth. . . . What shall we say to this? The scripture does not conceal it, and we dare not justify it. It was ill done, and proved of bad consequence; for it *occasioned the death of the priests of the Lord*, as David reflected upon it afterwards with regret. . . . David was a man of great faith and courage, and yet now both failed him, and he fell thus foully through fear and cowardice, and both owing to the weakness of his faith. Had he trusted God aright, he would not have used such a sorry sinful shift as this for his own preservation. It is written, not for our imitation, no, not in the greatest straits, but for our admonition.[2]

6. What was the difference between David's reaction to Ahimelech and his approach to the king of Gath and his men?

A few years ago, while digging into this text in 1 Samuel, I realized something. This movement from Ahimelech to Gath was really where David shifted from survival mode to speaking with God first about things. From here on out, his posture changed: He meditated and prayed to his Lord before acting.

Where are you turning to other people or your own strength during hard times instead of first going to God? Our best and most life-giving choice is to lean into Him, allowing Him to direct us and still our anxious hearts. We are not stuck in our pain. We can choose to say yes and listen to Him in the darkness.

Talk to God about the situations and ways in which you may be turning to everyone but Him. Ask Him to meet your heart in those places instead.

Amen.

WEEK 4 • *Day 2*

 READ 1 SAMUEL 21

Let's play a quick game. Is God more present at church than He is at . . .

home	Yes / No
work	Yes / No
the movie theater or gym	Yes / No
your favorite restaurant or hangout place	Yes / No
the mountains or beach	Yes / No

Of course not! God is everywhere. He's as present within the walls of a church as anyplace you go throughout your day. Here's what Psalm 139:7-12 tells us:

> Is there anyplace I can go to avoid your Spirit?
>> to be out of your sight?
> If I climb to the sky, you're there!
>> If I go underground, you're there!
> If I flew on morning's wings
>> to the far western horizon,
> You'd find me in a minute—
>> you're already there waiting!
> Then I said to myself, "Oh, he even sees me in the dark!
>> At night I'm immersed in the light!"
> It's a fact: darkness isn't dark to you;
>> night and day, darkness and light, they're all the same
>>> to you.

If this is true, then why do we walk inside our churches and expect to "feel" different? Why do we expect our prayers will be heard and answered more readily? Why are we so much more aware of God and His work in our lives (or our struggles) when we sit within the four walls of a church building?

1. Do you find yourself more in tune with God within the church walls than during the rest of your week? Why do you think that is?

_____

_____

_____

_____

_____

_____

Even as we acknowledge that God is omnipresent—that He's everywhere and can be worshiped from anywhere—we can live a very different story in our day-to-day lives, particularly if we are walking through painful circumstances. David (and the rest of the Israelites!) did this too.

Go ahead and open your Bible to 1 Samuel 21:7, where we learn that when David arrives in Nob, a man named Doeg the Edomite (Saul's head shepherd) is also there, "detained before the LORD" (ESV).

2. Before you start digging, what do you think *detained before the Lord* means?

_____

_____

_____

3. The word *detain* is the Hebrew word *'atsar*, which also trans-lates to say: *stayed, keep, retained.* Hmm . . . that doesn't really clear things up, so let's dig into the Hebrew and see what *before the Lord* means. Head to the BLB and click on the *Interlinear* for this verse. You may already know that the word *Yĕhovah* (יְהֹוָה, pronounced *yeh-ho-vah*) is a name for God, so let's move on to the word *before* (*paniym*; פָּנִים, pronounced *pah-neem*).

4. According to your *Interlinear*, what does *paniym* (פָּנִים) mean?

 History Lesson

When we dig into the word *before* (or פָּנִים; *paniym*), we learn that the presence/face/person of God was in this place. This is important, because while the Ark of the Covenant had at one time rested inside the beautiful Tabernacle these three men were visiting, it was no longer there. The Ark was designed to be a symbol of the presence of God living in the midst of His people—and yet He was still there when the Ark was not.

The wording in 1 Samuel 21:7 does not suggest that God forced Doeg the Edomite to stay in Nob but rather implies that he was detained, likely for one of several possible reasons:

• It may have been the Sabbath and therefore Doeg wouldn't travel on this day of rest.

- He may have committed some sort of offense and was detained until he had offered the appropriate sacrifice.
- He might have been there for purification after illness.

Whatever the reason Doeg the Edomite was at the Tabernacle, one thing is certain: He saw David without his usual entourage of soldiers, speaking with the priest. Verse 1 tells us that Ahimelech also noticed that David was traveling alone and trembled at the sight.

5. Why was this detail of note to both men? Why would David being alone make Ahimelech nervous?

David had reached a high rank in Saul's army and therefore rarely traveled alone. Whether he was on assignment from the king or on his own business, he would still have a group of men traveling with him. The fact that he didn't was disconcerting to Ahimelech and Doeg. By now, the kingdom would have known about the king's mood swings and how God had removed His blessing from Saul's kingship. The priest knew something was wrong if David was traveling in a manner unsuitable to his ranking.[3] While it's possible that David visited Nob because Ahimelech the priest was a safe person to go to, he may have also recognized this was more than just a little jealous spat with King Saul and wanted to see the Tabernacle one last time before heading into exile. But why didn't David tell Ahimelech the truth of what was going on?

6. Why do you think David fled to the Tabernacle? Why might he have covered his tracks with a lie?

There have been so many times when I've had every intention of trusting God and then, in the middle of the circumstance, wimped out and relied on myself instead of on Him. Have you ever been there? Wouldn't it be nice to know the consequences of our sins before taking that wrong step? We'd probably be less likely to continue forward if we knew the result of our lies and deception.

7. Why do you think God doesn't stop us from making those mistakes? What would we miss out on?

_____

_____

_____

_____

_____

_____

We often hear that God won't give us more than we can handle. Where did we get this idea? It's certainly not in the Bible! (Really, it's not . . . go ahead and check!) *Of course* God allows us to go through things that are too big or hard for us to handle. Why? Because He is God and He knows that even if we can't do it, *He can*!

In the horror of being forced to run for his life, David forgot the need to hold on to God white-knuckled and know that it wasn't in *his* own power but in *His* that things can be done. If we could do things ourselves, handle it all ourselves, how on earth would we ever realize we need God?

In fact, my sweet friend Lindsay Sherbondy has beautifully hand-lettered a canvas that says,

You are EXACTLY as STRONG as you think you are . . .
    IT'S GOD that will surprise you.[4]

Spend some time meditating on these words and this concept. Take your fears and uncertainties to God:

_____

_____

_____

_____

_____

_____

_____

_____

_____

Amen.

WEEK 4 • *Day 3*

📖 READ 1 SAMUEL 21–22

We're going to come back to Doeg the Edomite and why his seeing David was a big deal, but first, let's wrap up David's moments with Ahimelech the priest in 1 Samuel 21 and step into chapter 22. As we do, we're going to see how David cared for others even in the midst of his dark and difficult situation.

After being asked why he was alone in verse 1, David made up a story about being on a top-secret mission for the king and claimed that he was meeting the rest of his men nearby after securing food. His lie may have come from feeling unsure if he could trust the priest or possibly because he hoped to protect Ahimelech from Saul. Either way, his words alleviated Ahimelech's suspicion. Though the priest had no food to offer David but holy bread, Ahimelech gave what he had.

His question as to whether David and his men were ceremonially clean wasn't really the point—Ahimelech technically shouldn't have given the Bread of the Presence to anyone who was not a priest. But Ahimelech was a man of compassion, generosity, and kindness. He saw the bigger picture: David may not have been a priest, but he needed help. Generations later, Jesus even references this gracious priest in Matthew 12:3-7, praising him for understanding the need to put mercy before ceremonial law.

Fabricating an excuse that the king's business was so urgent that he left too quickly to grab his own sword, David also asks if the priest has a spear or sword to give. The priest responds,

> "The sword of Goliath the Philistine, whom you struck
> down in the Valley of Elah, behold, it is here wrapped in
> a cloth behind the ephod. If you will take that, take it, for
> there is none but that here." And David said, "There is none
> like that; give it to me."
>
> 1 SAMUEL 21:9, ESV

David left that very day and traveled to see Achish, king of Gath, as we read about in the last couple of weeks. After convincing King Achish of his insanity, David sets off again to a place where he knows he'll be safe for a while: the Cave of Adullam (which translates to "cave of refuge"[5]) in Judah. This cave, halfway between Gath and Bethlehem, was known to be fortified, providing a natural hiding place. (If you've not yet done so, read 1 Samuel 22:1-5.)

Because we're here to learn more about God by diving deeply, gaining insight using our own acumen and intelligence, let's do some digging to learn a bit more about this cave. We can understand history so much better after seeing photos or video or reading details. Google anything that helps you learn more about the Cave of Adullam (*Why is Adullam a good hiding place? David and Cave of Adullam*, etc.).[6]

1. Pen down three or four things that you find interesting about the Cave of Adullam:

   a._____

   _____

   _____

   _____

   b._____

   _____

   _____

   c._____

   _____

   _____

   _____

   d._____

   _____

   _____

The hiding place at Adullam was hundreds of feet above the valley. Caves were peppered around the hill, which was fortified on one side.[7] It even had a water source that flowed all the way down to the Dead Sea.[8] Like a little oasis in the desert, Adullam provided all David and his men would need: fruit trees, water, wildlife. Many of the caves even had openings that were hidden in the shadows and were spacious enough for large groups of men to live within. If you had to flee and live in a cave, this certainly seemed like a great spot to do so, right?

2. What else do we learn in 1 Samuel 22:1-2 about David's arrival at this hiding spot?

The Cave of Adullam might have been a great hiding spot; however, not only did David's family find him there, but many others did as well—vagrants, troublemakers, and other people who were discontent with Saul's leadership. The group grew to about four hundred men, and David led them all.

3. Why do you think these people came to David and gathered with him?

_____

_____

_____

_____

_____

I can just picture David hiding quietly, writing psalms in the caves, when suddenly he hears something outside. Gripping the massive sword that used to belong to Goliath, he quietly slips out to investigate. David quickly realizes that his father's household has arrived . . . and little by little, others begin to stream in, seeing themselves in his story. I wonder how David felt about that.

One of our kids has an awesome hiding spot for Hide-and-Seek. The other little kids discovered it, though, and have started trying to hide there too. It's pretty easy now to find four children all hiding behind a curtain, giggling as one whispers harshly, "Go find somewhere else!"

Do you think David wanted to tell these people, "Hey . . . this is my hiding spot! Go find somewhere else! You're too loud and there are too many of you—now they're going to find me!"?

4. Even in the midst of his profound struggle, David became a safe place for these vagrants and outcasts. What might that look like for us? To go through something devastating and yet remain kind, authentic, and encouraging through it? In fact, how do we become such a light *in the midst of* our struggles

that we also become a loving sounding board and safe place for others?

5. As we learn early on in chapter 22, "everyone who was in distress . . . gathered to him" (verse 2, ESV). How does David embracing these outcasts act as foreshadowing of how Jesus (who is often referred to as the Son of David) interacted with people here on earth?

6. Even David's own parents found him in Adullam. Why would they have left their home to come to this place filled with outlaws and others who were running from the king?

As word began to spread regarding Saul's hatred of David, his mother and father likely realized the possible threat to their own lives. To ensure their safety, David took them to Moab.

7. Does this seem strange? Why would David choose Moab, and how did he know they'd be safe there?

Moab was a country often in conflict with Israel, but it was a special place for David's family. Check out Ruth 4:13-22 to read a bit more about David's extended family.

8. Who was David's great-grandmother? _____

Do you remember Ruth's story? Ruth is the book directly before 1 Samuel, and it begins with a woman named Naomi fleeing to the country of Moab with her husband and two sons during a time of extreme famine in Judah (Ruth 1:1-2). Naomi's husband died. One of Naomi's sons married Ruth, who was a Moabite. But then both sons died too, and Naomi and Ruth left Moab to return to Judah.

9. Why is David's lineage significant here? (See Ruth 4:17 and Matthew 1:5-6.)

Since Ruth was David's great-grandmother, David's family had a blood connection with the people in the land of Moab. Because of this relationship, it was a good place to hide both David's mother and his father, Jesse. After receiving a warning from the prophet Gad, David parted ways with his family and went into the forest of Hereth (1 Samuel 22:5).

As we wrap up today, continue dwelling on how David cared about others despite his own difficulties. The king literally wanted him dead, and yet he invested in the safety of his family and the well-being of the four hundred men who came to him. David lived out God's love to them and built them into a great army. (Some of them even became the famous Mighty Men we read about throughout 2 Samuel—in fact, 2 Samuel 23 shares incredible detail about some of these men!)

David acknowledged that he wasn't the only one going through a painful season. We need to remember we're not alone in ours, either.

The details of our lives may be different, but the sadness, loneliness, and devastation are universal. We can say yes in the darkness as we are with and for each other, allowing ourselves to be vulnerable with our shared stories.

 Spend some time talking to God about how helping others could actually help strengthen you, too. In what ways could He use you through your struggle?

_____

_____

_____

_____

_____

_____

_____

_____

Amen.

WEEK 4 • *Day 4*

READ 1 SAMUEL 22

When David lied to Ahimelech at Nob, choosing to act out of fear instead of trusting God, he probably thought everything would be fine. His lie protected him, after all. Surely it wasn't a big deal. But when we depend on our own strength and decisions to get us through the darkness, we often miss the ways we can hurt other people. David learned this the hard way. Mistruths can sometimes lead to tragic consequences.

Today we're finally swinging back around to why Doeg the Edomite (Saul's shepherd) being detained in Nob was so important—and why his presence in that situation was so devastating. First though, let's read the rest of the chapter (1 Samuel 22:6-23).

1. How did Saul react when he heard David and his men had been discovered (1 Samuel 21:6-8)?

2. Who stepped forward to prove that he was loyal to Saul? What did this man tell the king (1 Samuel 22:9-10)?

What happens next is hard to read. The whole family of priests was summoned to see the king. I'm sure they were wide-eyed and trembling as they exited the Tabernacle, wondering if they were seriously supposed to just leave it without a priest. How curious other travelers must have been as they witnessed these eighty-five men—all wearing linen ephods, the beautiful sign of priesthood—journeying together down the dusty roads, heading toward the king and an unknown future.

3. As Ahimelech approached Saul, the king confronted the priest. How did Ahimelech respond to Saul in verses 14-15? (Note: I love how his answer was translated in *The Message* version. Read this first—available at BibleGateway.com if you don't own a copy—before looking at the passage in your favorite translation.)

King Saul disregards the priest's defense and orders Ahimelech and his whole family (meaning all the priests) to be killed, unintentionally fulfilling a prophesy in 1 Samuel 2:29-36. But the guards stand their ground and refuse to lay a hand on the men of God.

Furious, the king then turns to Doeg the Edomite, ordering him to kill the priests. The head shepherd obeys—and then goes even further.

4. Doeg displayed a deep fury and vengeance that the king didn't even request. After the priests were slaughtered, what did Doeg do?

_____

_____

_____

The entire town was murdered, down to the infants and animals. To give a bit of context, back in 1 Samuel 15, Saul refused to go this far even when God commanded him to—he preferred to keep the best cattle and such for himself. So allowing this action was above and beyond, even for the out-of-control king.

We could spend the rest of the week concentrating on the whys of Doeg's mass murder and try to understand why this head shepherd was actually such a skilled warrior, but instead we're going to go back to David. (You're welcome to dive deeper on your own, though—there are some really interesting theories on it all.)

5. Sum up 1 Samuel 22:20-23 in a sentence or two:

_____

_____

_____

In verse 22, David says to Abiathar (the lone escapee from Doeg's rampage),

I knew, when I saw Doeg the Edomite that day, that he
would certainly tell Saul. I am responsible for the death of
every person in your family.

VOICE

Can you imagine the guilt David must have felt? I picture him
falling to his knees, head in his hands, choking on grief and remorse,
as he finds out what happened.

I'm curious at what point David regretted stepping foot into Nob.
Was it here, as Abiathar told David about the horrors that occurred
and he realized the consequence of his lie? Was it the moment he
saw Doeg the Edomite and immediately had a bad feeling about it
all? Do you think that as he hid in that cave, he felt deep remorse
surrounding his lack of trust, even without knowing his hands were
stained with the blood of all of these people?

6. How do you think David felt?

Let's pause for a moment and ponder how David's lack of trust
in God, resulting lie, and subsequent tragic consequences apply to
us and our own lives.

7. When you're in a tight spot or in a place of pain or loneliness,
   do you act out of trust in God or out of fear? Do you remember to pray before taking your next step? Or do you often act
   first and realize later that you'd never taken the time to ask God
   for discernment and direction?

8. As you place yourself in David's shoes, reflect again about your trust in the Lord. When have you held fast and shunned fear, grasping tightly to His promise to remain by your side? When have you been in a situation where you didn't trust, and fear overtook you? What differences did you observe afterward?

The ways we act and the decisions we make when we're in a season of darkness don't affect just us. The people around us—our families, our friends, even the people we interact with at the grocery store—feel the ripple effects of our choices, good and bad. If we lie and hide in shame, our relationships suffer. If we're honest and vulnerable with God's work in the darkness, we can bring life to our interactions.

Spend some time of silence before the Lord. Pour out your heart to Him about the people walking alongside you in your hard situation. Listen to the quiet whisper He breathes on your spirit. How is your trust or lack of trust in God affecting the people around you?

Amen.

WEEK 4 • *Day 5*

 READ PSALM 52

You may be wondering how we've reached day 5 and haven't yet opened up this week's psalm. We needed to soak ourselves in the events and pain of the story David wrote out of so we can fully enter into the profound anger and grief he shares in this psalm. I suspect we'll read this psalm with different eyes now that we know the backstory.

1. Unlike many of David's other songs and poems, this one is directed not to God but to Doeg the Edomite. What do you think was David's purpose in writing it?

When our children are upset, they often write letters to my husband and me, leaving them on the kitchen counter, slipping them under our bedroom door, or taping them to my bathroom mirror. Sometimes they have a hard time verbalizing their hurt and anger and have found that the best way to get their heads around a thought or feeling is to write it all out. Are you that way too? I sure am.

That's exactly what David did here. Knowing he would probably never have the chance to confront Doeg face-to-face, he basically wrote a diary entry.

The psalm opens with David asking, *WHY?!* As he arraigns Doeg for his crimes, he's essentially saying, *Why would you do this, Doeg? For what purpose? Why do you boast of evil? For what reason does your tongue plot destruction? Why are you lying rather than speaking what is right?*

2. What did Doeg lie to Saul about?

_____

_____

_____

_____

Yes, there was truth in what Doeg told King Saul, but it was a half-truth. He purposely misrepresented the entire situation, distorting the conversation between David and Ahimelech the priest. Remember, David told the priest that he was on a mission from King Saul, which meant that Ahimelech was not intentionally defying the king. And yet Doeg the Edomite colored the story in a way that represented the innocent man as a traitor.

 ### *History Lesson*

These are the generations of Esau the father of the Edomites in the hill country of Seir.

GENESIS 36:9, ESV

In Hebrew, the word *'Edom* literally means "red."[9] And do you know where that name comes from? Esau, who was the eldest son of Abraham's son Isaac. As Genesis 36:9 tells us, Esau was "the father of the Edomites" (ESV). Esau has a few connections to the color red: he "came out red" when he was born (Genesis 25:25, ESV), and he sold his birthright to his brother Jacob for "red stew" (Genesis 25:30).

Doeg the Edomite was obviously from Edom. This foreign land was an enemy of Israel during the time of Saul's reign (1 Samuel 14:47), which tells us that Doeg was either a traitor to his own people or possibly a prisoner of war who had advanced himself into a high-ranking position.

3. We often tell our kids there are two kinds of lies: one of assertion, and one of omission. What's the difference?

Assertion: _____

Omission: _____

4. How were Doeg's and David's lies different?

_____

_____

5. In Psalm 52:4, David says, "You love all words that devour" (ESV). Head to the *Interlinear* in the BLB and write down the definitions for the term *that devour* (*belaʿ*; בֶּלַע, pronounced *beh-lah*).

_____

_____

As I read this description, the phrase *for ruin* catches my eye. *Ruin* is the heart behind Doeg the Edomite's deception. I'm in no way condoning David's lie, but his intent was to protect himself (and possibly to protect the priest). Doeg, on the other hand, was intentionally causing damage and hurt.

The problem with lying, no matter what the intent, is that it often snowballs out of control. That's what happened here. Both lies ended up in the same place: massive destruction. That's the hitch in dishonesty and deceit. Even when we think we're doing it for a good reason, justifying it to ourselves, it comes back to bite us (or those around us). It doesn't matter if our lies are full of assertion or omission, if they are half-truths or are in no way true. Convincing ourselves that our reason for it is justified, or that the smallness of it doesn't matter, is really just Satan lying back to us . . . omitting the truth that lies cause devastation and leave wreckage in their wake. Our reasoning for lying doesn't matter because we are simply commanded not to do it:

You shall not give false testimony against your neighbor.

EXODUS 20:16, NIV

In other words, God says we cannot lie to or about our neighbor—and truly, God considers everyone to be our neighbor. Jesus tells us that love of God and love of neighbor is the most important way we align ourselves with God (Mark 12:30-31).

Before the massacre of the priests and the town of Nob, Doeg posed as if he were in alignment with God. Matthew Henry's commentary says that "he attended the altars, and brought his offerings, and paid his respects to the priests."[10] In other words, Doeg the Edomite went through the motions of being devout to our heavenly Father.

There are so many people who consider themselves Christians because they, too, go through the motions:

- *Church on Sunday? Check.*
- *Tithe 10 percent? Check.*
- *Raise my hands in worship? Check.*
- *Say Christian-sounding lingo (Christianese) when chatting with other Christians? Check.*
- *I mean hey, I even brought my Bible with me and served in the nursery. I go to Bible study every week because I'm extra-committed.*

Obviously these are all great things . . . it's all stuff we might think we *should* do. But doing these is not what makes us a good Christian. In fact, not one or a combination of any of these things makes a Christian at all.

Do we raise our hands in worship because the people around us are or because we want it to look like we're super into it? Or do we raise our hands because we are in such unhindered love of Jesus that we open up our hands in surrender and adoration of all He is and has done? Do we tell the truth only when it's convenient? Or does God's love of us compel us to love others in authentic relationship, which means braving honesty even when it's risky?

In other words, it's not what we do and how we act; it's the heart behind it, the *why* in it all. We need to be honest with ourselves as we decide why we do these things: Do we want a deep relationship with Jesus, or are we simply working off some sort of "Christian checklist" we've created for ourselves?

Doeg apparently worked off this checklist and, as someone who had grown up with other gods, never actually understood what a love of God meant. Maybe he just went through the motions because he wanted to fit into life in Israel.

6. How might you be treating your faith more as a checklist than as a relationship? What does it look like to put Christ at the center, rather than concentrating on the to-do list of it all? How can you love your neighbor well out of that deep alignment with God's heart?

With Doeg's heart and motives as our background, let's dive into Psalm 52:5-7. These words are more than a little harsh. In fact, I find myself gripping my Bible with wide eyes and clammy hands, praying no one ever says something like that to me! I'm not big into scare tactics and screaming at people that they'll burn in the pits of hell if they don't follow God. I just can't see that as effectively showing the love and grace of Christ. But though David's harsh and blunt words here essentially tell Doeg that very thing, David isn't trying to scare him into following God. No—David is uncovering the bone-chilling truth of God's wrath against Doeg's atrocity and wants the man to understand the magnitude of his actions.

> But the Almighty will strike you down forever!
> He will pull you up by your roots
> and drag you away to the darkness of death.
> PSALM 52:5, TPT

David's proclamation that Doeg will be ripped up by his roots and dragged away is such a good reminder for us. Though we spend so much time becoming rooted in things here on earth—our families, our communities, our passions and jobs—they won't last . . . no matter how good some of these things may be!

Where are you rooted? Destroyers will be destroyed, and sadly, when Doeg was eventually plucked from earth, his eternity looked very different from one lived within the garden of the Lord. But when people love Jesus, "they are transplanted from the land of the living, on earth, the nursery of the plants of righteousness, to that in heaven, the garden of the Lord, where they shall take root for ever."[11]

I wonder if that's what David is getting at in verse 8 when he says he is "like a green olive tree in the house of God" (ESV).

One of our kids writes beautiful prose and poetry. Though he creates lovely visualization, half the time I need him to explain it for me because I'm just not comprehending the depth of what he's articulating. That's how I feel with David's magnificent poetry too. Let's dig in and figure out what he's intending to express here.

Grab your phone and open up the BLB, heading to Psalm 52:8. What does the Interlinear say about the phrase *But as for me, I am like a green* (in Hebrew, the word *ra'anan*; רַעֲנָן, pronounced *rah-an-ahn*)?

7. Write down the two describing words in the *Gesenius' Hebrew-Chaldee Lexicon* that have nothing to do with the color of the plant.

a. _____

b. _____

Do you see yet what David is saying here? I'm simply going to let you read what Charles Spurgeon wrote in reference to this verse because he puts it so beautifully:

> *"But I,"* hunted and persecuted though I am, *"am like a green olive tree."* I am not plucked up or destroyed, but am like a flourishing olive, which out of the rock draws oil, and amid the drought still lives and grows. *"In the house of God."* He was one of the divine family, and could not be expelled from it; his place was near his God, and there was he safe and happy, despite all the machinations of his foes. He was bearing fruit, and would continue to do so when all his proud enemies were withered like branches lopped from the tree. *"I trust in the mercy of God for ever and ever."* Eternal mercy is my present confidence. David knew God's mercy to be eternal and perpetual, and in that he trusted. What a rock to build on! What a fortress to fly to![12]

Saying yes in the darkness does not mean that we deny our pain. It means that we remain rooted deep in the Life-Giver, so that we can flourish even in the midst of destruction. As we do, we find ourselves more and more aligned with His heart—which in turn expands our love and care for others.

Using Psalm 52, write your own prayer or psalm to the Lord. Reach deep, dear friend. Take time with Christ. Listen to His whispers of how you, too, can flourish in times of trial and pain. Because I promise you, it is possible.

Amen.

WEEK 4 *Notes*

Share your biggest takeaways from this week:

Treasures in the Darkness

Psalm 63 + 1 Samuel 23–24

WEEK 5 • *Day 1*

 READ 1 SAMUEL 23:1-15

As his mania over David increased, Saul grew more and more neglectful of his true purpose as ruler of Israel. Instead, he became hyperfocused on David's imaginary crimes and how to find and kill him. At the same time, David pressed more and more into his relationship with God. Though this week's psalm is thought to be from yet another time David tucked himself away from Saul in a cave (1 Samuel 23:14-15), we're going to dig into the entirety of chapter 23 and even into 24. Remember, these are not disconnected stories, but a series of events all strung together!

1. In three sentences or less, what is this chapter about so far?

_____

_____

_____

_____

_____

2. Have you noticed anything different about how David handles the stress and terror of Saul hunting him down? What's different? (See 1 Samuel 23:2 and 4.)

_____

_____

3. What happens once David is in Keilah? (See 1 Samuel 23:10-12.)

_____

_____

_____

Over and over, David approaches the Lord in prayer for assistance, advice, and advocacy! Instead of coming to the Lord in the heat of the moment or even simply after the situation has passed, David is now approaching the Lord *before* acting.

4. Why do you think his approach to God has suddenly changed and grown?

_____

_____

_____

_____

_____

_____

_____

_____

_____

David has seen that his actions mean something. He has seen that people can be hurt (and killed!) because of what he does, where he goes, and with whom he speaks. Realizing he can no longer live in mere survival mode, he leans into figuring out how to thrive in his relationship with his heavenly Father, so others may thrive around him.

As we begin chapter 23, we learn that the Philistines were fighting against Keilah, looting the threshing floors. David reacted with urgency because the attacks would strip the people of Keilah of grain for the following year's crop. Isn't it interesting? Even though David was on the run, God tasked him with protecting the people from neighboring nations. We often think that God's heart for all people only appears in the New Testament, but here He is prompting the future king to care for people beyond his borders.

History Lesson

Wondering what a threshing floor *is*, exactly? Wonder no longer!

The threshing floor was an essential part of agriculture in the ancient Near East. Typically round, with a diameter of 25–40 feet (7.6–12.2 m), it was usually located near a village in an area exposed to wind. Once the farmer had selected the location, he cleared the ground of stones and compressed the soil until a firm surface resulted. When the "floor" was ready, he laid recently harvested sheaves of grain on it for threshing. The farmer then used large animals, such as oxen or donkeys, to pull heavy threshing sleds over the grain, separating the kernels from the stalks and husks. When the threshing was complete, a winnowing fork was used to toss the grain into the air. The wind blew away the lighter stalks and husks (chaff), as the heavier kernels fell back to the floor. The farmer sifted the kernels through trays to remove any dirt gathered in the process and then temporarily stored the grain in heaps on the floor or sealed it in jars for later use.[1]

The Bible says David "inquired of the LORD" (1 Samuel 23:2, ESV). The Hebrew word used here is *sha'al*, which means *beg, ask*, or *request*. So basically, though this situation needed immediate attention, David immediately stopped to pray.

What a difference from last week's study! As David ran from Saul first to Nob, then Gath, then on to Adullam and Mizpah, we don't hear of him stopping to talk to God at all. David didn't ask the Lord what His plan was, how he should handle things, where he should go, or who he should trust his life with. And because he went off using his own strategy, rather than trusting God with his circumstance, David's honor waned and people died.

Here in 1 Samuel 23:2, David prays and God answers, telling him, "Go. Attack the Philistines and save Keilah." When he approached his men with the Lord's instructions, they balked at God's direction, wondering how they could even consider going against Philistine forces in Keilah while living in hiding from Saul.

David went to God in prayer once again, this time possibly in front of his men, and asked for clarity in the direction the Lord had given.

5. Why do you think David stopped and went back to the Lord in prayer this second time, though God was supremely clear in what He wanted David to do?

David didn't inquire a second time out of skepticism. He had none! No, David came before the throne of God for the sake of his men. This is both the sign of a good leader and an indication that David's faith was continuing to grow.

For a long time, I was the queen of responding with, "I'll pray for you," when someone told me their struggles—and I never actually prayed for them. It's not that I didn't have every intention to. The promise just flew out of my head amid the busyness of life. I have a feeling I'm not alone in this! We have every intention to come before the throne on behalf of our friends or those in our community and yet . . . we just don't do it.

6. Do you struggle to remember to pray for others? How can you apply this story of David to your own experience?

The past several years, I've felt incredibly convicted about my forgetfulness and have started praying for someone right then and there, similar to what David does in this chapter. Quite honestly, sometimes it's awkward if I don't know the person well or if they're not the type who generally prays. But you know what? Not a single person has ever told me no.

And even if I don't stop and ask if I could pray for them aloud, I'll shoot up an *arrow prayer*, right then. If you've not heard that term before, it's basically shooting a quick yet direct prayer up to God. There's no fluff, no superlatives. It's simply something short and to the point like, *Lord, bring Andrea wisdom*, or *Father, help Kelly turn to You and away from fear*. It's amazing how one simple prayer will mark that person for me—and for whatever reason, I'm more likely to remember to pray for them again, outside of that conversation.

A few days ago, I was texting with a dear friend who shared that her husband admitted to having an emotional affair. I could have responded back with "Ohmygosh I'm so sorry" or something similar, but truly, I didn't know how to respond. I didn't feel like I had wisdom to share or advice to give. I love my friend and adore her husband and simply didn't have words to express my sadness for them. I felt like everything I could have said seemed flat and trite.

Instead, my texted reply said something like this:

Lord Jesus, You know the deep devastation felt in Lisa's[2] heart. You understand the crack that has formed in their marriage and relationship. I pray you would give them discernment, kindness, patience, and honesty as they begin to work out what comes next. Help them draw near to You as they take steps to heal and trust again, bringing You in as the strength and third strand of their marriage.

7. The Bible gives us all sorts of insight into how we can live out lives of prayer. Flip over to 1 Thessalonians 5:17 and write it down:

_____

_____

In this verse, Paul encourages us to . . .

- Pray continually. (NIV)
- Pray constantly. (VOICE)
- Pray without ceasing. (ESV)

8. How do you feel about praying without ceasing? What on earth might that look like?

_____

_____

Prayer isn't something we should limit to just our quiet time with God. Praying throughout the day means praying when a friend texts us in pain, when we're driving and dealing with anxiety, when we're worshiping and sensing God's nearness. Prayer can be specific and fervent, or we can come to God in such grief that we can't find words. Whether we speak aloud or allow the Holy Spirit to intercede for us in our wordless ache (Romans 8:26-27), we have access to the throne of God at all times. And when we lift thanks, requests, and adoration up to Him, He is actively listening to every word.

There are 86,400 seconds in a single day. Paul isn't telling us we need to literally pray all 86,400 of them. He is saying that we need to invite God into our everyday moments. We should act like David and pray before making decisions, talk to our heavenly Father about thoughts, ideas, and struggles, and thank Him for successes and blessings. Basically, we should just chat with Him throughout the day. Let's develop a lifestyle of saying yes in the midst of whatever we're facing by immediately turning to God.

 Talk to God about how you can begin praying before stepping out in action. And pray that the Lord would give you the courage to immediately pray for your friends, family, even coworkers. Whether you're asking if you can pray for them aloud or sending up arrow prayers on their behalf, talk to God about any apprehension or fears you have. Ask Him to give you boldness as you step into a life of constant prayer.

Amen.

WEEK 5 • *Day 2*

📖 READ 1 SAMUEL 23

Here in the beginning of chapter 23, David has faith in the Lord's direction, but his men do not yet have that same confidence. To help grow their assurance in their heavenly Father, David prays a second time—and God answers: "Go down to Keilah, for I am going to give the Philistines into your hand" (1 Samuel 23:4, NIV).

In obedience and faithfulness, David's company did what God asked, inflicting heavy losses on the Philistine army, ultimately defeating them and saving the people of Keilah. Saul caught wind that David and his band of outcasts were at Keilah and mustered his forces. He believed God was handing the young man over to him: "For David has imprisoned himself by entering a town with gates and bars" (1 Samuel 23:7, NIV).

But again David showed the strength of his trust in God. Instead of allowing his natural warrior instincts to kick in, he asked the Lord how to proceed. Once again, David was stopping to pray in the middle of crisis. And it's not like he went into a quiet room, lit some candles, put on some worship music, and lifted up his voice while dropping to his knees. Often prayer is in the middle of the battlefield of life. Kneeling in complete silence before the Throne of the Lord is obviously a great way to pray, but it's certainly not the *only* way to have conversation with our heavenly Father. David's prayer was likely in the heat of the moment, as the murmuring fear of his men grew louder.

Maybe it doesn't occur to you to stop and talk to God because you're so used to living alone in your hurt and existing in survival mode. Perhaps you're just going through the motions, or you've decided you don't need anyone and you've "got this." But God wants something different for you, something better. He wants to walk in it with you.

1. Read 1 Samuel 23:10-12 again and consider your relationship with God in light of David's relationship with God. What similarities do you see? What differences?

David and his men escaped the city before Saul's soldiers arrived, traveling all over, never staying in a single place for long. King Saul continued his manic hunt, changing course whenever he received new information about David's whereabouts.

When has God gotten you out of a scary situation like he took David out of (once again)? Perhaps you see a group of guys eying you from across the street as you hustle to open your car door. You can hear their comments and sense them walking toward you—but then they change directions suddenly, allowing you to jump inside, lock the doors, and speed away.

Or perhaps you were leaving your house one morning, only to get to the car and realize you'd forgotten your keys. After heading inside to grab them off the counter, you hustle back to the car and turn onto the busy road. As you do, you see a man drive through a red light, and you realize he likely would have hit you if you'd not run back in the house and been delayed those thirty seconds.

Both of those things have happened to me. I can think of time and time again where God's protective hand carried me out of situations that could have ended very differently. I'm not saying that bad things haven't happened and that the Lord doesn't allow difficulties and hardship. But we all experience times where He shows us He's ultimately in control, allowing and disallowing certain things.

2. I know it's easy to jump immediately to the times that we've gotten hurt and felt like God wasn't watching out for us, but let's remember the countless times God has given protection. Write about a time He's taken you out of a situation that could have ended so much differently.

Although David wasn't completely taken out of his hard situation, God continued to protect David from Saul. As we move into 1 Samuel 24, we see Saul learn that his adversary is hiding in the wilderness of En Gedi, and Saul gathers three thousand men to find him. That's when things get crazy. As they searched, Saul decided to relieve himself in a nearby cave—where David and his men happened to be hiding, out of sight, further in.

David's men urged him to seize the opportunity, and David did—sort of. He crept up behind Saul and carefully cut a corner of fabric from his robe without being noticed. But then—perhaps because he'd acted out of feeling pressure from his men rather than turning to God—David felt extremely convicted by what he had done. He called out to the king after Saul had exited the cave.

Open to 1 Samuel 24 and read the entire story.

3. What does King Saul do when David admits to what he did?

When he realizes that David had the opportunity to kill him and didn't, Saul suddenly understands that David likely isn't out to take his kingship after all—and, after all this time of chasing him, Saul recognizes David's kindness despite Saul's cruel hostility.

4. What do you think was going through David's mind during this exchange?

_____

_____

_____

Does David wipe his brow and do a little jig, thinking he can finally get on with his life? Nope. David isn't naive. He understands that jealousy has a horrible habit of ebbing and flowing like the tide. So he takes precautions and waits for real evidence that the king has changed. Sometimes bullies and abusers apologize and promise to change their ways, but unless a heart is truly moved toward godly repentance, an apology is actually just breathing space before the next strike.

You may be wondering, despite his precautions, why David genuinely couldn't understand Saul's jealousy. Years prior, when Samuel anointed young David at his father's house, we see no evidence that the old priest told the shepherd boy what he was being anointed for. Because there is no indication David had any idea he would become king one day, I'm sure he wondered why he was set apart—and why all of this was happening.

God certainly could have fashioned an easier course for David, one that didn't require so much fear and living in survival mode. But God needed to strip everything away from David to strengthen his character.

5. Where in your life do you feel like God has stripped things away? How might He be strengthening you in that?

_____

_____

_____

_____

One of my favorite quotes ever is by a woman named Dr. Elisabeth Kübler-Ross:

> The most beautiful people we have known are those who
> have known defeat, known suffering, known struggle,
> known loss, and have found their way out of the depths.
> These persons have an appreciation, a sensitivity, and an
> understanding of life that fills them with compassion,
> gentleness, and a deep, loving concern. Beautiful people do
> not just happen.[3]

6. How might we be more beautiful having gone through difficult
   things than if we hadn't?

David wouldn't come out of this season as the same boy who watched his father's sheep. In fact, he was no longer even the young, popular warrior and talented harpist. Through all the difficulty, he was becoming a man who clung tightly to God. A man full of perseverance, grit, and courage. Even when he did wrong, David always came back to God with a heart full of sorrow. Like us, David was fiercely imperfect but trying to be the person the Lord created him to be.

God had not forgotten David in the wilderness, and he hasn't forgotten us, either. God was preparing him for what was to come, teaching him to fight through the hard and through opposition.

David may not have known exactly what his calling was yet, but the battle against it had already begun. And when David lied and deceived, Satan won a round of battle. We will face opposition whenever God gives us a calling, whether it seems little or massive. Every. Single. Time.

During his time of running from Saul, David could have blamed God. He could have wavered in his faith as fear and doubt crept in. He could have said, "But I thought You were with me, Father! I thought You were good. I thought You would never forsake me. I must have heard You wrong. This is too much. Maybe You're gone, maybe You walked away . . . because this? *This, God?* This is too hard."

But he didn't. He continued to grasp tightly to his Father and fight. This season of massive difficulty drove him directly into his Father's arms. The Lord was teaching him to fight for his faith, for his men, and for his future. David learned how to do it honorably, with the Lord by his side. And because of this, he became a man of incredible spiritual strength.

Psalms 57 and 58 were written by David during this time of hiding from Saul, and as I read the first part of Psalm 57, I am reminded how we must do more than simply choose joy in difficult seasons. We must take it as a gift from God, grasping it tightly with both hands.

> Be good to me, God—and now!
>   I've run to you for dear life.
> I'm hiding out under your wings
>   until the hurricane blows over.
> I call out to High God,
>   the God who holds me together.
> He sends orders from heaven and saves me,
>   he humiliates those who kick me around.

God delivers generous love,
  he makes good on his word.
PSALM 57:1-3

> *Though our struggles are real,*
> *his faithfulness is* **more real***.*

 While Psalm 57 isn't this week's psalm, it perfectly fits what we're talking about today. Rewrite it here in your own words, fitting it into your own life and situation.

_____

_____

_____

_____

_____

_____

_____

_____

Amen.

WEEK 5 • *Day 3*

READ PSALM 63

Now that we've learned the backstory to this week's psalm, let's dive in to learn more about finding God's gifts in the midst of hardship. As our psalm opens, David is transparent about how exhausted he is. I can only imagine how bone-weary he must have felt, facing battles and leading hundreds of men, all while living a life on the run from a murderous king. The thing is, though . . . David's words here move beyond pure exhaustion to something more.

As your eyes pour over his words, circle the words, verses, and phrases that show how tired David is.

After you've done that, underline the words, verses, and phrases that show how encouraged and joyful he feels.

¹ O God, you are my God; earnestly I seek you;
    my soul thirsts for you;
my flesh faints for you,
    as in a dry and weary land where there is no water.
² So I have looked upon you in the sanctuary,
    beholding your power and glory.
³ Because your steadfast love is better than life,
    my lips will praise you.
⁴ So I will bless you as long as I live;
    in your name I will lift up my hands.
⁵ My soul will be satisfied as with fat and rich food,
    and my mouth will praise you with joyful lips,
⁶ when I remember you upon my bed,
    and meditate on you in the watches of the night;
⁷ for you have been my help,
    and in the shadow of your wings I will sing for joy.
⁸ My soul clings to you;
    your right hand upholds me.
⁹ But those who seek to destroy my life
    shall go down into the depths of the earth;
¹⁰ they shall be given over to the power of the sword;
    they shall be a portion for jackals.
¹¹ But the king shall rejoice in God;
    all who swear by him shall exult,
    for the mouths of liars will be stopped.

PSALM 63, ESV

I mean, did you basically underline this entire passage? It's kind of crazy, right? How in the world can someone in such a tough spot, who is obviously so over his head and weary of being in this particular season, be expressing such joy?

1. What is your favorite phrase or section of this psalm?

I have several favorites, but verses 1 and 2 really speak loudly to my heart:

> O God, you are my God; earnestly I seek you;
>> my soul thirsts for you;
> my flesh faints for you,
>> as in a dry and weary land where there is no water.

2. Have you ever walked through a time when you felt like your soul was faint—as though you were stuck in a "dry and weary land" without water? How did God meet you in that time?

A few years ago, I couldn't say these words. I was in survival mode. I was tapped out. I stopped earnestly seeking God, and in my exhaustion, I accidentally left Him behind. I wrote about it in my book *Beautifully Interrupted*:

> We were still so new to this whole adoption thing and were suddenly thrown into more transitions as Ben [my husband] began traveling back and forth from San Antonio

to Portland every month. . . . I look back on [this] as the most exhausting and overwhelming time of my life caring for and loving a four-year-old, a three-year-old, an infant, and our newest addition, a six-year-old who spoke almost no English. . . .

I remember collapsing onto the floor in the kitchen one afternoon and bursting into tears. As I sat there on the cold tile floor holding baby Imani, Anton and Laith both crawled onto my lap, cuddling and comforting me, while Ezekiel stared with wide eyes a few feet away. . . .

Lord, is this really what we're supposed to be doing? You've got to give me more strength for this! I absolutely cannot do it on my own. That day was a turning point for me. I certainly wasn't at rock bottom, but I was drowning. I needed to cling to Him tighter. I had to, or I wasn't going to survive. . . .

Though the very essence of my soul wailed at the notion of being so low that my tiny children were compelled to crawl on the ground to comfort *me*, the reality was that I desperately needed their unyielding love while sobbing on that floor. And at that moment, God also bestowed their sweet tenderness to remind me of Himself. That His love is also unyielding and tender.

As I ugly cried on the floor, being cared for by my precious preschool-age children, God whispered the word *firstfruits* into my ear.

. . . *Firstfruits?* I asked, confused. *Help me understand what You mean, Lord!*

I knew that firstfruits are offerings of the first and best crops to God, which is often spoken about in the Old Testament. It was an offering given in acknowledgment of God's abundant blessing. Definitely not giving Him what is left over, but rather giving Him the best of the best *first*. . . .

What was I giving Him? The leftovers. The leftovers of my time, my energy, and my heart. He was reminding me of the need to put Him first. Above everything. . . .

. . . I needed to lean into the Lord and live in a posture of humility. . . .

I felt the Lord direct me, saying to give my firstfruits during naptime. Rather than scurrying through the house cleaning up, doing laundry, and tackling the constant stream of dishes, I was called to *first* sit and be with Him. Then do my tasks *after*.

And it changed everything.

. . . Jesus loved me back to life. My season changed.

Somehow I was receiving a divine amount of ability and productivity. The Lord was multiplying my time, renewing and energizing me. I could see His hand in my life as my patience grew. Grace was extended toward our family and kindness was electrified. Magnified. I was more attentive and loving, and my tasks were not only being completed but being executed thoroughly, and well. And through it all, I confidently leaned on Him, knowing it was in His power, not my own, that it was all getting done.

. . . I'm not going to lie and tell you that I suddenly turned into Mother Teresa or walked around with a halo over my head, never complaining when the kids spilled their milk for the fourth time that day.

I still prayed daily that God would work in me to give me a good attitude, patience, and strength so that I wouldn't lose my temper with my family because things weren't as perfect as I wanted them to be. But as my time of intimacy increased, my whole being began to blossom with fruit. The storm that I felt was going to drown me instead made me stronger because it led me back to Him.[4]

Have you been in a similar place of feeling overwhelmed and tapped out? Life can be like a tsunami, crashing over you. The good, the hard—it's all just too much.

3. How can you use both David's perspective on joy and the principle of firstfruits to help in your current season . . . or in preparation for the next time life gets to be too much? List several ideas:

a. _____

_____

_____

_____

b. _____

_____

_____

c. _____

_____

_____

_____

d. _____

_____

_____

Joy is not something we can manufacture. But God can do something miraculous in us when we choose to offer Him the firstfruits of our lives instead of dragging ourselves to His feet when we've reached the end of ourselves. A few years ago, I heard Beth Moore say[5] something about how joy is a gift that's handed to us by the Lord. It's available—we simply need to let Him give it to us. As we see in today's passage, David understood this. Even in the face of difficulty, he was able to still take joy from our heavenly Father, who leans down to place it into our weary hands—if we're willing to take it.

Let's end our time together in prayer. What might God be asking you to give Him? Or what might He be trying to give you?

_____

_____

_____

_____

_____

_____

_____

_____

_____

_____

_____

Amen.

WEEK 5 • *Day 4*

 READ PSALM 63:1-5

As we began to read Psalm 63, we easily sensed that David's tone was one of joy and refreshment even though he was exhausted and weary. How did he do that? And how can *we* do that?

I was reading through Matthew Henry's commentary today, and I was struck by this observation:

> This psalm has in it as much of warmth and lively devotion as any of David's psalms in so little a compass. As the sweetest of Paul's epistles were those that bore date out of a prison, so some of the sweetest of David's psalms were those that were penned, as this was, in a wilderness.[6]

Like David, the apostle Paul was targeted and pursued. No stranger to being imprisoned for sharing a message of Jesus' love and resurrection, Paul was honest in his struggle but also had an extravagant amount of joy pulsing through his veins—even when it didn't make sense.

Let's turn to 2 Corinthians 11 and look at verses 25 through 28, where Paul talks about all the sufferings he's lived through.

1. How many times did each of these things happen?

    _____ beaten with rods

    _____ stoned

    _____ shipwrecked (a night and a day he was adrift at sea)

2. What other dangers did he talk about living through?

    Ex. On frequent journeys,

3. Can you even believe all the hard things Paul experienced? And yet what does he say in the first part of 2 Corinthians 11:12 (ESV)?

    I will _____

4. Why does Paul say this? (Hint: Read 2 Corinthians 11:10-14.)

So basically, Paul is so in love with Jesus and committed to the message He brings to the world that Paul would gladly suffer if that meant people would know the One True Savior. In the same way, David's love for God infuses him with joy even in the midst of being pursued by Saul.

5. If you experienced even half of the things Paul or David did, would you still believe in God's goodness? Would you still love Him? Why or why not? (Be honest! This is for you—no one else needs to see your answer if you'd rather not share it.)

_____

_____

_____

_____

_____

_____

Back in Psalm 63, verse 3 says:

Because your steadfast love is better than life,
    my lips will praise you.
ESV

Incredible. David isn't blaming God for his struggle, he isn't yelling at Him, even though he knows God could snap His fingers and end Saul's single-minded pursuit of David. Even though it sure sounds as if Saul plans to no longer pursue the former shepherd (1 Samuel 24:17-21), David knows he can't believe him (which is smart because Saul's change of heart ultimately . . . wasn't real). And yet there is no anger here. No accusation, no criticism, no diatribe.

David simply states, "Your steadfast love is better than life, and

I will praise you." Wow. So what *is* steadfast love, and how does it overcome the power of David's pain?

Let's take a look. Head to the BLB and open the *Interlinear*, clicking on the phrase *Your lovingkindness* (another translation of *steadfast love*) in Psalm 63:3.

6. What does this word *checed* (חֶסֶד, pronounced *kheh-sed*) mean?

With this word, David is thinking of who God is at the very core of His character. Instead of focusing on the difficult realities of his physical life, David reflects on his spiritual life. Verse 4 goes on to say:

> So I will bless you as long as I live;
>   in your name I will lift up my hands.
>
> ESV

When someone lifts up their hands in worship, it's a sign that they are focusing wholly on God and coming before His throne in surrender. David realizes that this sign of devotion can happen not just within the walls of the sanctuary but anywhere. True worship is not about the circumstance and location but about the position of the heart.

Corrie ten Boom was a woman who loved Jesus and didn't waver in strength, forgiveness, and love of God even through the most horrible experiences during the Holocaust. As I reflect on David's posture of trust and worship in the midst of awful circumstances, I'm reminded of something Corrie wrote:

> If you look at the world, you'll be distressed. If you look within, you'll be depressed. But if you look at Christ, you'll be at rest.[7]

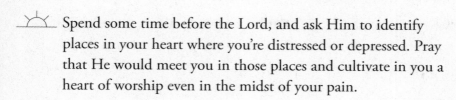 Spend some time before the Lord, and ask Him to identify places in your heart where you're distressed or depressed. Pray that He would meet you in those places and cultivate in you a heart of worship even in the midst of your pain.

Amen.

WEEK 5 • *Day 5*

 READ PSALM 63:6-8

When I was young and couldn't sleep, my dad would always tell me to do one of two things:

- *Read your Bible.*
- *Pray.*

At the time, I'd roll my eyes—those were about the last things I wanted to do. If I couldn't sleep, I may as well read my favorite book or watch a movie, right? Or at the very least, I thought, I should get to play with my toys until my eyelids were heavy. Who wants to read that boring Bible or pray . . . that'd put me straight to sleep! *Ohhhhhhhhhhh*, I thought. *That's why I should do those things!*

I chuckle now every time one of our kids taps on our door late at night, rubbing their eyes, complaining that they, too, cannot sleep. I say the same thing my dad once did. Except now, I understand why he suggested it.

Head to BibleGateway.com or YouVersion.com and scroll through a few translations of Psalm 63:6-7 (perhaps start with the ESV, NIV, NKJV, and end with VOICE and TPT).

 ### *History Lesson*

The Israelites didn't measure time in hours like we do—they measured it in groupings. No, not like how some of us measure our day with *breakfast time*, *lunchtime*, and *dinnertime*. Or even *evening*, *night*, and *please-don't-wake-me-up* time or *first cup of coffee, second cup of coffee, third cup of coffee* (which is how I gauge my day, sometimes . . .). The Israelites measured the night by three military watches, or periods of time when guards were on duty. The first watch (Lamentations 2:19) was from sunset to 10:00 p.m.; the middle watch (Judges 7:19) was from 10:00 p.m. to 2:00 a.m.; and the morning watch (1 Samuel 11:11) was from 2:00 a.m. to sunrise.

Later in Israel's history (specifically, during Roman times), they moved to four watches, which ended at 9:00 p.m., midnight, 3:00 a.m., and 6:00 a.m. These watches were either referenced by numbers (first, second, third, and fourth) or by titles ("even," "midnight," "cock-crowing," and "morning"; see Mark 13:35).[8]

1. Rewrite Psalm 63:6-7 in your own words, or combine your favorite word translations from various versions.

_____

_____

_____

_____

_____

_____

I absolutely love the way Charles Spurgeon expands on verse 6 (you can find it in the BLB under _Text Commentaries_[†]):

> He turned his bedchamber into an oratory, he consecrated his pillow, his praise anticipated the place of which it is written, "There is no night there."

My husband, Ben, teases me about falling asleep about a half second after my head hits the pillow. I go-go-go all day, and by bedtime, I absolutely crash. But some nights, especially if Ben is out of town, I wake up in the middle of the night and struggle to fall back to sleep. Most of these wakings are moments I know 100 percent that God is withholding my slumber because He's asking me to spend time with Him. And, as Spurgeon so beautifully explains, I, too, turn my bedchamber into an oratory, lifting up friends and family, struggles and fears, and thanking Him for his protection, guidance, and love. In the same way, when I was young and my dad encouraged me to read my Bible or pray when I couldn't sleep, what he was actually doing was helping me understand that I can approach the throne at any time, night or day.

[†] On the BLB website, you can find this under _Study/Commentaries_; on iPhones, it is labled _Commentaries_.

2. What do you do when you can't sleep?

Do you think perhaps these are moments when God is asking for some time with you? That He wants you to tell Him about the stresses wrapping you up so tightly that sleep doesn't come easily? What if your eyes are open because He wants you to trust Him with your struggles and pain, as much as your happiest joys?

3. Think back to a recent time you struggled to sleep. What kept you up? How might you take that before God?

David's yes in the darkness is often in the literal darkness. Day or night, no matter the difficulty, he wants a close and honest relationship with his heavenly Father. We see another expression of this in Psalm 63:8.

> My soul clings to you;
>   your right hand upholds me.
> ESV

This chapter has several references to *hands* and *lifting up*. Verse 4 talks about David lifting up his own hands, and now four verses later, he's talking about God's.

4. Why do you think David singles out God's right hand? Why specify a certain hand?

Several of our children are from a country where hands—instead of utensils—are used for eating. In that country, the right hand is the "clean" hand, used for things like eating, writing, and shaking someone else's hand. The left hand is used for . . . well, let's say less-clean things like using the restroom. If I were in Ethiopia and said I'd hold someone up with my left hand, they would be less than excited. Reaching out with my right hand is much more honoring because of what each hand represents.

The same symbolism was true in Hebrew culture.[9] David knows God wants the best for him. He wants to honor David and love on him as He holds him up at times when David cannot stand on his own.

 ## History Lesson

In ancient times, a person with high or the highest rank stood to the king's right side. Even today, a person may be called someone's "right-hand man (or woman!)" or "wingman" when he or she serves as the closest person to another leader. An example of this can be found in Genesis 48:13-14, when Jacob blessed the child who would receive a greater blessing with his right hand. The right hand of God likewise relates to this concept of someone being right next to God, acknowledging both authority and closeness to Him.[10]

Let's look and see what the word *upholds* literally means in the Hebrew text. Head to the BLB and go to Psalm 63:8, clicking on the *Interlinear*.

5. What other words do you read for *tamak* (תָּמַךְ, pronounced *tah-mak*)?

6. In what way(s) might God hold you up or support you?

Have you ever needed to be held up because you're too weary to go on? God can hold us up in many ways, but one that feels especially personal is when He holds us up by using people around us.

A story in Exodus gives us a vivid example of how our friends can hold us up when things get to be too much. The Israelites were fighting for their lives against the Amalekites, and ahead of the battle, Moses relayed God's instructions to Joshua:

> "Select some of our best men, and go fight against the soldiers of Amalek. Tomorrow I will stand at the crest of that hill overlooking the battlefield with God's staff in my hand."
>
> Joshua did exactly as Moses had instructed him to do. He gathered the strongest men he could find and fought against the soldiers of Amalek. Meanwhile, Moses, Aaron, and Hur climbed to the top of the hill.
>
> EXODUS 17:9-10, VOICE

But then the men around Moses observed something:

> It happened that whenever Moses raised his hand, the battle went well for Israel; but whenever he lowered his hand to rest, Amalek began to win. When Moses became too tired to hold his hands up any longer, Aaron and Hur took a stone and sat him down on it. Then both men stood beside Moses, one on each side, holding his hands up and keeping them steady until sunset. In the end, Joshua and the men of Israel defeated Amalek and his soldiers with the sword.
>
> EXODUS 17:11-13, VOICE

Now those are discerning friends who knew they needed to step up and into action. Have you ever experienced this?

7. When has someone close to you held you up in a difficult season? What was that experience like?

_____

_____

_____

☼ As we close, let's meditate on the poem below. Write in the lines next to it and have conversation with God as you reflect on the words.

One night I dreamed a dream. _____

As I was walking along the beach with my Lord, _____

Across the dark sky flashed scenes from my life. _____

For each scene, I noticed two sets of footprints in the sand, _____

One belonging to me and one to my Lord. _____

After the last scene of my life flashed before me, _____

I looked back at the footprints in the sand _____

I noticed that at many times along the path of my life, _____

especially at the very lowest and saddest times, _____

there was only one set of footprints. _____

This really troubled me, so I asked the Lord about it. _____

"Lord, you said once I decided to follow you, _____

You'd walk with me all the way. _____

But I noticed that during the saddest and most troublesome times of my life, _____

there was only one set of footprints. _____

I don't understand why, when I needed You the most, You would leave me." _____

He whispered, "My precious child, I love you and will never leave you, _____

Never, ever, during your trials and testings. _____

When you saw only one set of footprints, _____

It was then that I carried you." _____ _Amen._

AUTHOR UNKNOWN

WEEK 5 *Notes*

Share your biggest takeaways from this week:

Stepping into Darkness

Psalm 51 + 2 Samuel 11–12

WEEK 6 • *Day 1*

 READ 2 SAMUEL 11:1-2

We're going to jump ahead in the life of David this week, to a psalm and a story that circle a particular season of darkness. So far we've been exploring the kind of hard situations we all so often face: the ones without explanation, the ones that feel out of our control. But David's life shows us another kind of darkness—the self-inflicted kind. Sometimes we choose to step into sinful choices that have consequences, and the pain of those decisions can be profound. And this week, we're going to learn what saying yes to God looks like even then.

This is our first time digging into 2 Samuel; Saul has passed away (1 Samuel 31), and David is officially king. This book of 2 Samuel shares the story of David's reign over Judah and Israel and spans approximately forty years: from his ascension to the throne, when he was around thirty years old, to the end of his life. What's interesting, though, is that the book itself is divided exactly in half—meaning that the first twelve chapters celebrate David's achievements, victories, and triumphs, and the last twelve document his tragedies as the wheels fell off this flourishing kingdom.

The first twelve chapters show a time when David is walking in alignment with God. With the Lord's help, David led military campaigns that drove away invaders and brought incredible prosperity to the land. The last twelve chapters, though, record rebellion, deep pains in his family life, and even civil war. Toward the end of the book, David runs for his life once again. This time, however, it's from his son Absalom, who attempts to snatch the throne from his father.[1]

What on earth happened to David at that halfway point in the book? Chapters 11 and 12 show us the reason for David's decline.

David is no longer being hunted, he's no longer hiding in caves, no longer hungry, cold, and uncomfortable. His kingship is one of wealth, prestige, comfort, and success. I'm not saying he doesn't work hard or that he's just sitting around having women peel grapes and feed him all day. And I'm certainly not implying he's too busy enjoying life as king that he's not leading the Israelites whom he loves and has responsibility to guide and protect (or am I?). What I am saying is that there's a possibility he simply got comfortable. And often, comfort leads us astray.

Let's turn to 2 Samuel 11 and read verses 1-5.

Yep—we're at the beginning of the story of David and Bathsheba. Every time I read this legendary drama, I can hear Jeff Buckley's famous cover of Leonard Cohen's song, "Hallelujah":

> *Well, your faith was strong but you needed proof*
> *You saw her bathing on the roof*
> *Her beauty and the moonlight overthrew ya . . .*[2]

If you've heard the rest of the story, then you know that her beauty certainly did overthrow him. But why was he on the roof, anyway?

1. In verse 1, what does it say happens in the spring?

During the season when the kings went out to battle, David remained at Jerusalem. Apparently, David sent everyone else out to ravage the Ammonites and besiege Rabbah, choosing not to lead his forces into battle himself.

Spring fighting wasn't a religious or cultural thing; it was simply practical. Generally, war didn't happen in the winter because the conditions were too hard on the men. In the spring, the rain (or in some cases, snow) had begun to ease up and paths could be reopened for chariots. Ample food was available from the springtime wheat and barley harvests, as well from animals they came across as they moved from place to place conquering.[3]

Although it wasn't unheard of for the king to not go to war with his men, this decision was very unusual for David. He was a warrior, making his strategy, experience, and leadership invaluable. His choice to remain in Jerusalem is a bit of a head-scratcher, and the fact that the writer of this book pointed it out shows how unusual it was.

So why on earth was he home? Perhaps the battle against the Ammonites was expected to be an easy win and David felt Joab could handle it alone. Maybe David didn't feel like going out into the harsh life of war, or he was weary and exhausted from the duties of kingship. Maybe he just wanted a little downtime.

2. Why do you think David remained behind?

Whatever the reason, David wasn't where he was supposed to be. And because of that one seemingly small choice, David made decision after decision that led him even further outside of the will of God.

In 2 Samuel 11:2, we read,

It happened, late one afternoon, when David arose from his couch and was walking on the roof of the king's house, that he saw from the roof a woman bathing; and the woman was very beautiful.

ESV

Really, David? You were chilling on your couch in the afternoon? I looked up the word *afternoon* in the *Interlinear* and discovered that it's listed as *evening*. Confused about the discrepancy, I scrolled down to the lexicon, where I learned that it meant "first evening," which is apparently how the Hebrews described when the sun was beginning to descend. So, basically, in the late afternoon hours,

David was relaxing on his *mishkab* (bed or couch). I wonder how long he'd been reclining there? It seems weird, doesn't it? For a king to just be hanging out and relaxing during the work day?[4] I mean, how often do you sit on the couch late in the afternoon? Rarely, right? And you're not even running a nation!

I really do wish we had more information here. But let's assume the best of David here—maybe he was simply overwhelmed, exhausted, and completely tapped out. Because you know what? I've totally been there, and I have a feeling you have been too.

When I'm especially weary, I say no to what I'm supposed to be doing. Yes, it's healthy to say no to many things. But what about our essential responsibilities, commitments, and callings?

One of our kids is on an incredibly competitive soccer team. Soccer is his first love and his passion. Being on this team is his dream come true, and we committed to supporting him as a family. He plays six days a week and travels out of state and abroad for games, and depending on traffic, getting to practice each evening can take forty minutes one way.

What happens if I'm too exhausted to tackle the forty-minute drive in horrible traffic, the hour-and-a-half wait while he sweats it out on the field, and the long drive home in the dark? What if I skirt my responsibility as a mom, don't take him, and just stay home? I'd be telling my child that the commitment I made to him wasn't one I actually took seriously. I'd be teaching him that you can skirt responsibility when life gets to be too much. I'd be letting him down, and I'd be letting his team down.

3. What are your essential responsibilities? How can you discern what you need to say yes to versus what you're free to say no to?

It's easy to get so busy with the hustle of the everyday, with everything we feel we should be saying yes to, that we forget we need to be filled up. We pour our heart into our jobs, our families, our friendships, and various other responsibilities. Society today holds busyness as a badge of honor! The thing is, though, "busy" often leaves us feeling completely depleted.

That's where David was. For whatever reason, he seemed tapped out, unwilling or unable to live into his larger calling. His response to that depletion devastated the trajectory of his future and the future of many others around him.

4. Have you ever walked into a wrong decision out of exhaustion? In what ways can you identify when you're depleted?

_____

_____

_____

_____

The good news is, depletion is not a foregone conclusion. When we recognize the dangers of living from that place, we can seek God's guidance to point us toward restoration.

When I was relatively new to Denver, I felt like I had no friends in my city. God began encouraging me to stop waiting for people to invite me over and invite *them* over instead. I began inviting women over for playdates, lunch, coffee, book club, Bible study, and all sorts of other reasons—really, anything I could think of as an excuse to open my door. It was during that time that I realized how exhausted and depleted *so many* of us were. Out of that, I started hosting an annual event: *Let's Party Like Girls*. It's an evening for depleted women to be filled up; in fact, over time, the tagline became "Let us replenish you . . . so that you can pour out."

We dress up in ways we usually don't—that cocktail dress from the back of the closet, the leather or sequined pants that never get pulled out. We put on red lipstick and heels, and for some of us, it's simply taking the extra time to blow-dry and curl our hair. The goal is love and restoration on many levels: fun things like signature drinks and treats and giveaways alongside deep conversations about purpose and making a difference in the lives of others without getting too tapped out. As part of that pursuit of purpose, we work with nonprofits to remind ourselves that when we are full, we have the capacity to pour out to others.

Women leave feeling beautiful, seen, and appreciated. They leave feeling filled up. Replenished. And from that, they're able to pour out to others.

5. What are some things that fill your soul when you're feeling tapped out?

Author and researcher Brené Brown addressed depletion in an interview about her research on shame and vulnerability: "One of the things I found was the importance of rest and play, and the willingness to let go of exhaustion as a status symbol."[5] We must find channels that bring us life and ways for our cups to be filled because we cannot thrive in a place of depletion. God longs to help us find rest so that we can live out of abudance, not lack. Will we let Him?

As we conclude today, take some time to talk to God about being where He wants you, rather than where you've decided to be.

Amen.

WEEK 6 • *Day 2*

 READ 2 SAMUEL 11:3-5

As we read on in 2 Samuel 11 today, things go from bad to worse. David saw Bathsheba bathing on her roof, sent his men to retrieve her, slept with her, and then sent her away.

Can you imagine getting that knock on the door? Culturally, there was nothing she could do about his request: He was king, and she was to obey. The thought makes my heart drop.

Bathsheba would have known David well. Perhaps not personally, but because the men in her life worked intimately with the king, she would have grown up hearing conversation and recounted stories from her father, grandfather, and husband.[6] We know from reading through other areas of the Bible that Bathsheba's family was highly esteemed by David himself. In fact, her father Eliam (2 Samuel 11:3), also known as Ammiel (1 Chronicles 3:5), was ranked as one of David's thirty-seven Mighty Men (2 Samuel 23:34). The Mighty Men were essentially commandos on par with or even superior to the special ops and elite forces of today. These men conquered in hand-to-hand combat and engaged in covert military operations, often in the face of staggering odds (2 Samuel 23:8). And yet time after time, they stood their ground and ended up being the last men standing.

Bathsheba's grandfather Ahithophel was the chief counselor of the king, ranked even higher than the priests Abiathar and Jehoiada (1 Chronicles 27:33-34). His counsel was so wise, in fact, that 2 Samuel 16:23 says, "The counsel that Ahithophel gave in those days was treated as if God himself had spoken."

These men, whom Bathsheba had known since birth, loved and trusted the king. They gave their lives in support of him, as did Bathsheba's husband Uriah (we'll get to him a bit later).

The problem is, sometimes people we trust betray and hurt us. And when that happens, life can change forever.

I had coffee with a friend this week, and we were talking about how heartbroken we both are about what some friends are currently going through. I cannot even tell you how many women I know who have recently found out their spouse was unfaithful. These men, many of whom I adore and have known for years, are having affairs, are addicted to porn, are lying about late nights or business trips, and have even simply said family and children are "too much work" and "this is not for me." Betrayal leaves devestation in its wake.

1. Have you gone through incredible betrayal? Or has someone close to you, perhaps? Share it below. Don't worry about details; just be vulnerable with your heart's hurt and anger.

We know that disloyalty, deception, and extreme lapses of judgment happen. Those things, sadly, are not surprising. What *is* surprising, though, is when it happens *to us*.

Betrayal drops us off at a fork in the road where we have two choices: become stuck and brood over it for years, allowing it to slowly rip apart our entire life, or decide to do the hard work to heal and move forward. We get to decide which path to take, though admittedly one will require a lot more effort than the other. But the harder road is the one that will ultimately leave us empowered and whole.

When betrayal comes, we go through many cycles of grief. We often battle a little voice that whispers that we did this or caused this. Let me be clear . . . whatever betrayal you are facing is *not* your fault. The betrayer made a choice, and you are absolutely not to blame for that decision.

David was someone Bathsheba should have been able to trust—the trusted leader of her nation, beloved in her family. But instead he used his power and proximity to take advantage of her. She was bathing on her roof, but she was certainly not doing it in the open. In those days, in fact, houses were built with a tall wall surrounding the rooftop patio, so people in nearby houses could not peer over and watch as someone bathed. Let's look at how *The Voice* translates verse 2:

> Early one evening, David rose from his bed and was strolling
> on the palace roof when he saw a woman bathing on a roof
> below his.
>
> 2 SAMUEL 11:2, VOICE

Did you catch that? David's palace was higher than the nearby houses, so he had a completely different viewpoint.[7] Because of this, he had a perfect bird's-eye view of Bathsheba's bathing.

2. Was Bathsheba being indecent?

_____ Yes

_____ No

Why or why not?

_____

_____

_____

Bathsheba was going through the purification process from her uncleanliness (2 Samuel 11:4), which means she had just ended her monthly period and was performing the ritual that allowed her to join society once again (learn more about this aspect of the Mosaic law in Leviticus 15:25-30). She did nothing wrong. But even if this had happened after she stood in the town square and bathed for all to see, King David would still be at fault.

We all have free will and are responsible for our own actions. You cannot force someone else to sin—they have to choose it. You are not to blame for someone else's betrayal.

That being said, however, we can always seek to be wise, walking and living in a way that protects us from the invasion of a betrayer. A while back, a friend told me that someone else got credit for her brainchild. She had worked months on this idea and its creation, but because two heads are better than one, she brainstormed with a friend and colleague. What did this other girl do? She released a mirror-image product mere days before my friend. Guess whose product is killing it and whose isn't because it looks like the copycat? Yeah. That stinks, right? My friend now knows that, as silly as it seems, she must have people sign an NDA (nondisclosure agreement) before sharing information on unreleased products, brainstorming, and collaborating with anyone else—even friends. Her boundaries have now been set so she's not hurt like this again.

How about you? Are there places in your life where you need to set clearer boundaries and stick to them? Have you blindly extended trust that was unearned? Do you tend to ignore obvious signs of trouble in order to avoid conflict? Awareness is a powerful thing, and identifying our blind spots is important for understanding how to guard ourselves from those who might inflict this kind of pain.

Of course, these questions won't apply to every situation. Bathsheba did nothing wrong by bathing on the roof, and she had no culpability in the aftermath. The fault for everything that followed lay completely at the feet of King David.

So how do we process and heal in the aftermath of a betrayal we never saw coming? We have no idea if Bathsheba had someone safe and trusted with whom she could talk through this heartache, but I hope she did. No one should wade into deep hurts alone.

3. Who would you (or do you) go to during hard times? What characteristics show they're a safe person to share your secrets with?

After writing that description of your go-to safe person, I want you to think of yourself. Underline the words that others might apply to you. Be honest here—you don't need to share this with anyone else. Are you a trusted friend? Can people come to you with their heartache?

4. In what ways do you communicate trustworthiness? Are there any ways in which you may seem unsafe or unapproachable?

I want to point out that sometimes we're in a place where we don't have someone to use as confidant. Someone I know recently told me that because she's seen as the fun life-of-the-party, she's always invited out to go clubbing or to fun events around town. The problem is, when her boyfriend began beating her, she had no one to talk to about it. She had people to go out and party with, but when life came crashing down around her, she felt completely alone. Those relationships only went as deep as what was going on that next weekend.

If that's you and you don't know whom to pour your heart out to in a safe and healthy way, I urge you to find a counselor. Or beeline your way over to a pastor at your church (or any church!) next Sunday. Even if you don't feel like they're the right person to share it all with, simply tell them you're really struggling and were wondering if they could help you find someone to speak with. I guarantee they will bend over backward to help. You can also reach out to prayer lines through many ministries. Focus on the Family, for example, has both prayer and counseling resources.[8]

Betrayal is devestaing, and it cannot be undone. You may not have wrapped your mind around where to go from here, and I understand that deeply. But whatever you are going through, you are not alone. Your betrayer does not have the final word. Our God is a God of restoration, and He will restore the broken pieces of your story.

Spend some time with the Lord, earnestly praying that He show you how to move forward and begin to heal. It will take work and time, but cling to Philippians 4:13: "I can do all things through him who strengthens me" (ESV). Remember also what we talked about in week 2: He gathers up your tears (Psalm 56:8). You are not alone in this, no matter how much it feels like you are.

Amen.

WEEK 6 • *Day 3*

 READ 2 SAMUEL 11:6-27

Yesterday we talked about what happens when we're the one who is betrayed. But what about when we are the betrayer?

While in my twenties, I dated a guy who (behind closed doors) was emotionally and verbally abusive. I was so wounded that when a guy I worked with spoke kindness and encouragement over me, I didn't know how to handle it. Instead of breaking up with my boyfriend, I cheated. The fact that I'm even saying this out loud to anyone other than my family and best friend means that the Lord has done a lot of hard work helping me heal from the incredible shame that surrounded that short yet destructive season of lies.

I was the betrayer, and it still pains me to have done what I always said I'd never do.

1. Have you ever betrayed someone's trust? What was your internal and external response in that situation?

2. Has your heart healed from the devastation you caused, or are you still struggling with shame because of it?

_____

_____

_____

_____

_____

Today in 2 Samuel, we look at David, this man who has spent so much time leaning into God and learning to depend on Him . . . now becoming the betrayer. Let's unflinchingly look at this hard story. Each of us is susceptible to shame and sin that ends up hurting everyone around us.

3. What did David do in 2 Samuel 11? Write a T for True or F for False in each square:

☐ Was working hard doing exactly what he should as king

☐ Saw a beautiful woman bathing and immediately turned around, knowing he shouldn't look, and desired instead to be a man above reproach

☐ Forced a married woman to sleep with him

☐ Was honest in his sin and immediately expressed remorse, asking for forgiveness

☐ Lied so many times it snowballed into something he didn't know how to get out from under

☐ Had someone killed/murdered

David's desperate attempt to smooth over this horrible situation only made matters worse as the lies compounded. Have you ever found yourself stuck in that kind of vicious cycle? I once watched a show where the wife made the husband meatloaf once a week for years upon years because when they were newly married, he had fibbed and told her how much he loved it. The funniest part? She hated meatloaf too. So for decades, they both gagged their way through a dinner they didn't enjoy, fake smiling all the while.

4. What's the problem with even small-seeming white lies?

5. Have you ever been stuck in a cycle of compounding lies? What was the impact on your life and relationships?

Just as David's lies began to snowball, ours will too. We tell ourselves that a tiny lie isn't a big deal—and little by little, we get comfortable with those tiny-seeming lies. Suddenly, bigger ones become okay as we justify to ourselves that they're "not that bad." Like the proverbial frog in the pot of water, we don't notice that our surroundings are boiling until it's too late.

If you've had a long day and just feel like staying in to watch a movie instead of wading through traffic and going to dinner with a friend as had been planned, a fib like "I'm sorry I can't hang out tonight, I'm just not feeling well" may seem okay. But what's the true heart *behind* such lies?

6. What's the *real* reason you sometimes tell a mistruth? Check all that may apply:

☐ cowardice—the fear of hard conversations and confrontation;

☐ selfishness—the intentional or unintentional belief that what's going on with you is more important than the effect your lie has on the other person's life;

☐ perfectionism—the desire to make yourself appear a certain way;

☐ pride—the unwillingness to admit when you need help or when things aren't going as well as you want others to think they are (a very close friend of perfectionism); and/or

☐ greed—doing what it takes to get what you want because of an overwhelming desire for more.

7. What other, deeper reasons tempt you to lie?

_____

_____

_____

A few years ago, I heard a speaker tell the story of a man who had just gotten out of prison. Walking aimlessly, without a place to go or anyone to talk to, the man came to a church and decided to go inside. He quietly made his way up to the front pew and sat and stared at the Ten Commandments, which were written in beautiful gold paint behind the pulpit.

As he read, the commandments that used to feel like demands suddenly felt like kind promises. Rather than reading an accusatory "You shall NOT LIE!!!!!!" yelled over him, the man sensed a gentle assurance: "With Me, you shall not lie." In other words, God opened his eyes to understand the heart behind the commands.

I am reminded once again that if David had been seeking God, this story of Bathsheba would never have been written. But because the king's eyes wandered off his heavenly Father and onto a naked woman, and then onto self-preservation, things collapsed around him. God longed for him to choose differently—and how much different things would have been had David sought God's heart and walked away from the darkness of deception and betrayal.

But even if, like David, we choose the path of pain and sin, that is not the end of the story. Actions are what we do—not who we are. We have lied; we are not a liar. We have deceived; we are not a deceiver. We can choose to walk away, to change our actions, to ask for God's forgiveness and step into a life of truth, kindness, honesty, and peace—no matter how far gone we may feel. Because we're never too far for God. Nothing—not even our sin—can keep us from His offer of love and forgiveness.

Ask God to surface any places in your life where you have allowed deception or betrayal to rule your actions. Pray that He would meet you in those places and walk with you into truth and repentence.

Amen.

WEEK 6 • *Day 4*

 READ 1 SAMUEL 12:1-15 & 2 SAMUEL 12:1-15

Are you wondering why in the world I've taken you all the way back to 1 Samuel in our reading today, to the chapter where Samuel is bidding the nation farewell and publicly passing the torch of leadership onto Saul? Well, just bear with me—I promise it's important for understanding David's yes in the darkness of 2 Samuel 12. Because this is the turning point of this whole horrible story: what David decides to do when he's finally confronted with his sin. And we can really only understand how important his choice is in light of another king's sin—and another king's choice.

In 1 Samuel 12, the prophet Samuel reminds the Israelites that even through generations of their repeated acts of turning from God, He has never left their side (1 Samuel 12:6-11). The Lord never abandoned them but instead allowed pressure from their enemies so they might turn back to Him for help. And though Saul is their leader, God is still their Great King:

> If you will fear the LORD and serve him and obey his voice
> and not rebel against the commandment of the LORD, and
> if both you and the king who reigns over you will follow the
> LORD your God, it will be well.
>
> 1 SAMUEL 12:14, ESV

Samuel doesn't say that life will be easy. None of us are promised that life will be happy, peaceful, and comfortable at all times. But this verse says if we follow God, *it will be well.*

Several verses later, Samuel returns to this crucial point:

> Only fear the LORD and serve him faithfully with all your
> heart. For consider what great things he has done for you.

But if you still do wickedly, you shall be swept away, both you and your king.

1 SAMUEL 12:24-25, ESV

Samuel wanted to make sure they grasped this: As a nation, the people of Israel needed to first and foremost love and follow their heavenly King. These people had seen how idolatry, turning away from God, tore their nation apart before. Their history was a reminder of how *not* to act. Samuel urged them to look to the future, worshiping God only. Trusting Him above all. Saul began his reign fully understanding the importance of Samuel's words here. He actually started out as a humble and good king! But over time, he allowed himself to grow comfortable in his luxurious palace.

If you remember, when God removed his blessing from Saul, Samuel reminded Saul of what God really wanted from him: "obedience is better than sacrifice" (1 Samuel 15:22, VOICE). Sadly, Saul had apparently decided he was done with that fact. He was so convinced of his own greatness that his moral compass was skewed. He'd forgotten that God wasn't on the same level—that God is King and Supreme Ruler . . . and Saul was just the leader of a small land in the Middle East.

1. Why is it important for us to remember Saul's journey, in light of what we're studying about David this week?

2. Head over to 2 Samuel 12:1-15. Write a quick recap of these verses:

Just as Saul came to a crossroads in his leadership, so did David. They both started off as humble men and got comfortable. Entitled. And sin entered in. But here's where things get interesting: How they responded to being convicted of that sin couldn't have been more different.

3. What's the difference between how Saul and David responded to their sin?

SAUL'S RESPONSE (1 SAMUEL 15:17-31)	DAVID'S RESPONSE (PSALM 51)

Both kings were confronted by their prophet-advisers, who held them accountable for their immorality and iniquity. Neither king knew at the time, but how they responded had bearing on their future reign. God would either continue to bless, or He would remove that blessing.

4. Why do you think God handled them so differently, though they were both apologetic?

God knows the heart behind all we do and say. Saul only apologized when the consequences became clear (1 Samuel 15:28). David received the rebuke from Nathan and immediately repented. God could tell the difference between the hearts of these two men.

Because David came to the Lord with a contrite and grieving heart, God restored him. There were certainly consequences to be had, but God's presence—His Spirit—remained with him.

In the days of the Old Testament—generations before the death and resurrection of Jesus and the outpouring of the Holy Spirit—the Holy Spirit would come onto certain people for a particular purpose (e.g., Exodus 31:2-5; Numbers 27:18; Judges 3:10). In the days of David, when God removed His blessing from someone, He also removed His Spirit.

5. How is this different from the Spirit's role when we sin today?

If you love me, show it by doing what I've told you. I will talk to the Father, and he'll provide you another Friend so that you will always have someone with you. This Friend is the Spirit of Truth. The godless world can't take him in because it doesn't have eyes to see him, doesn't know what to look for. But you know him already because he has been staying with you, and will even be *in* you!

JOHN 14:15-17

Different versions translate the word for Holy Spirit in this passage slightly differently, though all obviously mean the same thing. For example, *The Message* uses the word *Friend* and the ESV uses the word *Helper*. Let's dig into this a bit.

6. Head to John 14:16 in the BLB and click on the word *Helper*, heading into the *Interlinear*. This word *paraklētos* (παράκλητος, pronounced *pa-ra-klay-tos*) means a lot more than just *Friend*.

After reading through the *Outline of Biblical Usage* and/or the lexicon, how would you describe *paraklētos*?

"One who pleads another's case before a judge" and "called to one's side"[9]—that almost sounds like a defense attorney, right? We also see words like *advocate, intercessor, helper, assistant, adviser,* and *counselor.* I know these are supposed to clarify and allow us to see deeper into who the Holy Spirit is and what He does, yet I feel like each of these words is lacking in fully grasping this aspect of the Trinity.

The notes section in *The Passion* version of this passage says,

> The translator has chosen the word *Savior,* for it depicts the role of the Holy Spirit to protect, defend, and save us from our self and our enemies and keep us whole and healed. He is the One who guides and defends, comforts and consoles. Keep in mind that the Holy Spirit is the Spirit of Christ, our Savior. The Aramaic word is *paraqleta,* which is taken from two root words: (1) *praq,* "to end, finish, or to save," and (2) *lyta,* which means "the curse." What a beautiful word picture, the Holy Spirit comes to end the work of the curse (of sin) in our lives and to save us from its every effect! *Paraqleta* means "a redeemer who ends the curse."[10]

7. After reading those notes and definitions, how would you describe the Holy Spirit's work in our lives?

David may have responded differently because he remembered what happened with Saul and wanted to ensure his life didn't emulate that of his predecessor. But this week's psalm (which we'll dig into more tomorrow) points to his more profound concern:

> May you never reject me!
> May you never take from me your sacred Spirit!
> PSALM 51:11, TPT

More than simply being afraid of losing his kingship, David craved the Lord and was devastated that his wrongdoing could separate him from a relationship with his heavenly Father. And even out of horrifying sin, he could still turn back to God. The same is true for us: Even when we ignore the Holy Spirit's promptings, we are never so far from Him that we cannot get back. He is calling us to return, to repent, to choose life. Will we listen?

The evil one's voice of shame can be loud—but God is always, always calling us home. Are you struggling with sorrow, fear, shame, disappointment? Bring that to Him now. Let Him breathe life back into you as He spreads a cloak of forgiveness and love over your shoulders. Say yes to Him, no matter how much you feel like you don't deserve another chance to live for Him:

Amen.

WEEK 6 • *Day 5*

 READ 2 SAMUEL 12:15-23 & PSALM 51

Whether you're a parent or not, this portion of the story likely grips your heart hard. Bathsheba's sweet, innocent baby boy becomes sick shortly after his birth, and I imagine the color draining from David's face as he realizes he is facing the prophesied consqeuences of his actions. Another death because of David's actions. I wonder if the king's mind flashed back to the tragedy of the priests from Nob being massacred years prior, also because of his actions (1 Samuel 22).

Psalm 51 is David's cry of pain and repentence after he chose sin upon sin in the situation with Bathsheba. And from him we can learn what it looks like to come before God with the hardest, darkest part of our stories—and be met with grace.

1. What does David immediately do in response to the realization that his infant son is ill?

2. Please read Psalm 51 in your favorite translation and write down a few emotions you feel David is sharing through this psalm:

3. I wonder at what point David penned the words of Psalm 51.
   When do you think it was?

☐ after lying with Bathsheba (2 Samuel 11:1-4);

☐ after hearing that Bathsheba was pregnant with his child
   (2 Samuel 11:5);

☐ after the conspiracy behind and death of Uriah (2 Samuel
   11:6-25);

☐ after David's eyes were opened by Nathan's parable (2 Samuel
   12:1-9);

☐ after his infant son became ill (2 Samuel 12:15-17);

☐ after his son passed away (2 Samuel 12:18-19); or

☐ (other) _____

4. Why do you think that's when he wrote it?

_____

_____

_____

No one knows exactly at what point during the events of 2 Samuel
11–12 David sat down with parchment and quill to write Psalm 51,
but it's widely thought that he wrote it soon after the conversation
with Nathan. As this prophet and friend confronted him, using a
parable to get through the king's thick skull, David's blinded eyes
were opened to the truth and the gravity of what he had done.

Different translations of Scripture passages hit me in different
ways. For me, Psalm 51 really comes alive in *The Voice* version. I'm
including it here, but go ahead and use whatever translation speaks
to you the most for this particular passage.

[1] Look on me with a heart of mercy, O God,
   according to Your generous love.
According to Your great compassion,

wipe out every consequence of my shameful crimes.
² Thoroughly wash me, inside and out, of all my crooked deeds.
Cleanse me from my sins.

5. What is David's attitude and emotional state as he comes to the
Lord in Psalm 51:1-2?

David seems broken and humble, doesn't he? He seems to recognize that he doesn't deserve forgiveness but is pleading for it even
so. This might be hard for us to swallow—that David could sin so
seriously, and profoundly hurt so many people . . . and that still God
would forgive him (though David would still face some very serious
consequences). But shouldn't that also encourage us? God is ready to
forgive the one who repents, no matter what we have done.

³ For I am fully aware of all I have done wrong,
and my guilt is there, staring me in the face.
⁴ It was against You, only You, that I sinned,
for I have done what You say is wrong, right before
Your eyes.
So when You speak, You are in the right.
When You judge, Your judgments are pure and true.
⁵ For I was guilty from the day I was born,
a sinner from the time my mother became pregnant
with me.

Wait a second. Psalm 51:4 says, "It was against You, only You,
that I sinned." But weren't a large number of other people devastated
by David's actions? Bathsheba, Uriah, Joab (Uriah's blood was ultimately on Joab's hands), David and Bathsheba's baby. Even Nathan,

Bathsheba's father Eliam (I mean, helloo . . . wouldn't you be more than a little frosted if you were her father?), Bathsheba's grandfather Ahithophel. Ahithophel eventually sides with David's son Absalom a little later when Absalom tries to take over the throne. I wonder if Ahithophel's decision was influenced at all by David's treatment of his granddaughter?

6. What do you think David means when he says, "It was against You, only You, that I sinned"?

David obviously hurt a slew of people. We can assume that friends, family, and the whole nation balked with horror at what their God-fearing king had done. David is not trying to downplay that here; rather, he's emphasizing that God's judgment and opinion of him are of immense importance. Ultimately, it was not man's perception but God's that David cared most about. He knew that he was born a sinner (verse 5), and that from his very first breath, he (and we as humankind) struggled with striving to live in a way that is perfect and blameless . . . and missing the mark over and over again.

> 6 But still, You long to enthrone truth throughout my being;
>   in unseen places deep within me, You show me wisdom.
> 7 Cleanse me of my wickedness with hyssop, and I will be clean.
>   If You wash me, I will be whiter than snow.
> 8 Help me hear joy and happiness as my accompaniment,
>   so my bones, which You have broken, will dance in delight
>   instead.
> 9 Cover Your face so You will not see my sins,
>   and erase my guilt from the record.

¹⁰ Create in me a clean heart, O God;
  restore within me a sense of being brand new.
¹¹ Do not throw me far away from Your presence,
  and do not remove Your Holy Spirit from me.
¹² Give back to me the deep delight of being saved by You;
  let Your willing Spirit sustain me.
¹³ If You do, I promise to teach rebels Your ways
  and help sinners find their way back to You.

Some of David's language might seem a bit over-the-top as he tries to express the depth of his grief over his sin. Did you read verse 8 and think, *Wait a second, are David's bones broken? Where's* that *in the story?*

Here's the thing: David isn't saying he needs a cast because God literally fractured his bones. What he's trying to express is that when he knows God is disappointed and saddened by his behavior, that pain penetrates his entire body, down to his very bones. He feels broken inside.

7. What makes you feel broken inside? Have you ever felt that in your relationship with God?

---

¹⁴ Free me from the guilt of murder, of shedding a man's blood,
  O God who saves me.
    Now my tongue, which was used to destroy, will be used to
    sing with deep delight of how right and just You are.
¹⁵ O Lord, pry open my lips
  that this mouth will sing joyfully of Your greatness.
¹⁶ I would surrender my dearest possessions or destroy all that I
    prize to prove my regret,
  but You don't take pleasure in sacrifices or burnt offerings.

17 What sacrifice I can offer You is my broken spirit
 because a broken spirit, O God,
  a heart that honestly regrets the past,
You won't detest.

Reread that last verse (Psalm 51:17). What a mic-drop moment, right? David knows God intimately. There may be loads we will never comprehend with our earthly minds, but this much is unwaveringly certain: God loves a contrite heart. He doesn't love that we're in the position of deep remorse, obviously. But when we choose not to blame anyone else, when we avoid coming up with excuses or getting defensive, when instead we're genuinely saddened and repentant—that makes God supremely happy. He loves when we're teachable and open to His leading.

8. How would you reword verse 17 to fit with you and your life?

18 Be good to Zion; grant her Your favor.
 Make Jerusalem's walls steady and strong.
19 Then there will be sacrifices made,
 burnt offerings and whole burnt offerings,
With right motives that will delight You.
 And costly young bulls will be offered up to Your altar, only
  the best.

Don't throw out this last section because it feels unrelatable. Because of Christ's death and resurrection, we no longer take part in the practice of burnt offering, but these words are still for us.

9. What do you think is the heart behind David's promise to make sacrifices?

_____

_____

_____

_____

_____

If you're completely bewildered, don't fret. I absolutely love how my *ESV Study Bible* explains this part of the psalm:

> The psalm closes by enabling worshipers to see the relationship between their own spiritual health and the well-being of the whole body of God's people (**Zion**). That is, each member is linked to all the others in a web of relationships, and together they share in the life of God as it pulses through the whole body. Thus each member contributes to (or else detracts from) the health of the whole. The ideal Israel is a community of forgiven penitents, faithfully embracing God's covenant and worshiping him according to the rites he appointed; this is the community that can bring light to the whole world.[11]

Just as the Israelites of the Old Testament were God's chosen people, so are we, the modern-day believers in Jesus. We are the "ideal Israel" as we embody a community of repentence and forgiveness. Out of our darkness—even our self-inflicted darkness—we can "bring light to the whole world."

When one of our boys was ten, he started making his own candles to "shed light" on the global water crisis, saving up to fund a water project. He named his company *Light of the World Candle Co.*, and each candle jar has Matthew 5:14-16 written on it in *The Message* translation:

Here's another way to put it: You're here to be light, bringing out the God-colors in the world. God is not a secret to be kept. We're going public with this, as public as a city on a hill. If I make you light-bearers, you don't think I'm going to hide you under a bucket, do you? I'm putting you on a light stand. Now that I've put you there on a hilltop, on a light stand—shine! Keep open house; be generous with your lives. By opening up to others, you'll prompt people to open up with God, this generous Father in heaven.

Our son loves the wording of "the God-colors," this vibrant idea of our light helping others see the brilliance of God. So how do we each bring out the God-colors in the world? We are to open up to others. We are to share our stories—even the stories when we were the liar and the deceiver, and God rescued us from our own darkness. I'm not saying we need to stand on the hilltop to gossip and share intimate details that aren't anyone's business but our own. But I will say that the Lord put you there on that hilltop to be His light for the world. Shine brightly! Take the time and do the hard work to heal. And stand tall, knowing that just as He has used David's story for His good purpose, He will also use yours.

Ask God how the hard seasons of your story could be transformed into opportunities to show His loving goodness. Can you come before Him with gratitude that He is so good at bringing light to your darkness?

Amen.

WEEK 6 *Notes*

Share your biggest takeaways from this week:

Saying Yes

Psalm 18 + 2 Samuel 22

WEEK 7 • *Day 1*

 READ PSALM 18 & 2 SAMUEL 22

Since we just came from studying and dissecting David's short-comings with the house of Uriah last week, it may take a minute to bounce back and remember that he really was a good man and great king—so much so that we know God Himself calls David "a man after My own heart." This week's story and psalm are an opportunity for us to reflect on what we've learned about David's life—as he himself reflects back on the ups and downs, valleys and mountaintops, the choices that pushed him further from God and the ones that drew him closer. How does a man at the end of his days process a lifetime of saying yes in the darkness?

1. Taking a few minutes to flip through our past weeks, let's write down words that define David's character, phrases to explain his heart, and anything meaningful to you through this study (for help with this, check out your notes at the end of each week):

Week 1:

Week 2:

Week 3:

Week 4:

Week 5:

Week 6:

Now that we've spent some time reflecting on David's journey (and our own!), we're going to move through this week at a bit of a different pace. Put your finger or a bookmark on both Psalm 18 and 2 Samuel 22. We're going to flip back and forth a little bit to learn what a relationship with God looks like after a lifetime of yeses.

2. Read 2 Samuel 22:9 and write it below:

_____

_____

_____

3. Now flip to Psalm 18:8 and write it below:

_____

_____

_____

4. Now head over to 2 Samuel 22:4 and write it below:

_____

_____

_____

5. Flip back to Psalm 18:3 and write it below:

_____

_____

_____

These passages are crazy similar, right? Though the wording is nearly identical, these two passages were created for different purposes. In 2 Samuel 22, David is simply journaling, expressing appreciation and gratitude to the Lord who loved him through a life full of challenges. The text in Psalm 18, however, adapts David's personal declaration into a song for the entire nation.

6. In the same way that David's personal time with God became an anthem for a nation, God's words and work in someone else's life can resonate deeply in our own. What words or principles passed on from someone else have helped define your own life and perspective?

_____

_____

_____

_____

Let's zoom out just a bit to discover where we find David in these passages. In 2 Samuel 23, we read David's official farewell and last words, which means that in 2 Samuel 22, he is now old and gray. He's certainly lived a very full life of incredible highs and massive lows, and this royal psalm, Psalm 18, is meant to honor both the Davidic monarchy and God Himself. The people are to sing the psalm in celebration of the way God has shown His love to the Israelites and for His protection of David. Because their future is tied to the health and well-being of David's heirs, the nation would sing this song in thankfulness while praying that the kings to come would be men of valor who fought fiercely for their country and for a heart after God, just as David did.

Because 2 Samuel 22 and Psalm 18 nearly mirror each other, we will often be using them interchangeably this week. For example, if we're digging into a word in Hebrew, know that the word or phrase will be translated the same way no matter if it's from 2 Samuel 22 or Psalm 18. And if we look into culture or history for one passage, we can assume that it explains the other passage as well. Make sense? Great!

7. Before we wrap up this first day of our last week, let's reflect back on our previous weeks one more time. Has learning more about David's story helped you step toward consistently saying

yes to Him, even in the dark times? What have you learned so far about saying yes in the darkness of your own story?

_____

_____

_____

 Spend some time with God, and ask Him how He wants you to say yes to Him today:

_____

_____

_____

_____

_____

_____

_____

_____

_____

_____

Amen.

WEEK 7 • Day 2

READ 2 SAMUEL 22 & PSALM 18

Our boys love to wrestle with my husband. Like, *love* to wrestle with him. When one of them was around seven or eight, he would always exclaim in somewhat broken English, "Daddy, you like a *rock*!" He'd say it in such awe and admiration, with a big rolling *r* because of his gorgeous Ethiopian accent. When I read 2 Samuel 22:2-4, that's how I read it, with my heavenly Father being an incredible *rrrrrrock*. He is solid. He is someone I can trust because He is unmovable. And that's a big part of saying yes to Him, right? Knowing that He can't be shaken by anything we're walking through?

> [2] The Lord is my rock and my fortress and my deliverer,
>   [3] my God, my rock, in whom I take refuge,
> my shield, and the horn of my salvation,
>   my stronghold and my refuge,
>   my savior; you save me from violence.
> [4] I call upon the Lord, who is worthy to be praised,
>   and I am saved from my enemies.
>
> 2 SAMUEL 22:2-4, ESV

1. Let's head to the BLB and dig in a little bit here. What are the words for *rock* in verse 2 and verse 3?

I have searched commentaries and googled extensively and simply cannot figure out why there is a difference. The only thing I saw is from a Jewish question-board, someone asking the same thing. The rabbis on the board referenced different passages than we're covering here, but I think their responses also answer our question: David was trying to show his maturity in understanding the depth of God's strength.[1] Let me explain:

- **verse 2:** The Lord is my rock (*cela'*; סֶלַע, pronounced *seh-lah*) and my fortress and my deliverer,

- **verse 3:** my God, my rock (*tsuwr*; צוּר, pronounced *tsoor*), in whom I take refuge, my shield, and the horn of my salvation, my stronghold and my refuge, my savior; you save me from violence.

One rabbi referenced a long discourse (thankfully translated into English) that talked about Moses calling water from a rock. Two different times, the Old Testament shares about him doing so, though God asked him to do it differently each time. The first time, God tells Moses to *strike the rock* to make water flow out (Exodus 17). Many years later, God tells Moses to *speak to the rock*, commanding water to come forth (Numbers 20). Moses doesn't listen this second time and instead hits the rock two times. From it, the water still flowed, but his lack of obedience and grandiose manner of drawing out the water kept him from the Promised Land.

Rabbi YY Jacobson explained that צוּר (*tsuwr*) is used when the Jewish nation was still considered "young," and forty years later, as Moses and the Israelites neared the end of their wandering through the desert, they had reached the level of a סֶלַע (*cela'*):

> Before any refinement could be achieved [in the newly freed people of Israel], the outer "rock" needed to be cracked. The "hard skin" they developed over 210 years in exile, needed to be penetrated before its inner vibrant and fresh waters could be discovered. . . . At this primitive point in Jewish history, smiting the "rock" was appropriate, indeed critical. Their hearts were too dense to be pierced in any other way.[2]

Later, he goes on to say,

> The model of smiting must be replaced with the model of teaching and inspiring. . . . Moses, who came to identify so deeply with the generation he painstakingly liberated from Egyptian genocide and slavery and worked incessantly for their development as a free and holy people, could not easily "change his skin" and assume a new model of leadership. . . . He continued to employ the method of rebuke and strength.

And he struck [the rock] twice, because when you attempt
to change things through pressure, rather than by persuasion,
you must always do it more than once. . . .

. . . Moses belonged to the older generation. Because
of his profound love and attachment to that generation
. . . Moses did not possess the ability to properly assess the
transformation that had taken place in the young generation
of Jews. . . . That is why G-d told Moses, "You did not have
faith in Me, to sanctify Me in the eyes of the children of
Israel."[3]

2. How could this interpretation influence our understanding of
   David's words in 2 Samuel 22?

Because there's not a broader consensus in how to interpret these
words, we can't know for sure—but I do wonder if King David was
trying to show that he, too, had matured. That he was once young
in his understanding of God as *tsuwr*, and now, after years of growth,
he knew him in a much deeper way (*cela‘*). In other words, verse 2
showed who he believed God to be as he wrote the chapter and
verse 3 gave his impression of God as He became his *refuge, shield,*
and *Savior who protected him.*

Does the word *rock* (*cela‘*; סֶלַע, pronounced *seh-lah*) remind you
of anything else? If you've read many of the psalms, you've probably
noticed the word *selah* (pronounced the same as our rock—*cela‘*),
which exists even in our English translations. *Selah* is used seventy-
one times in the book of Psalms (and three in the book of Habakkuk).

Since David was a musician and poet, I wonder if he was using creative license with the sounds of the words, and perhaps if that might also explain why he used this term *cela'*.

3. Please head to Psalm 46 in the BLB and click on the word *selah* (verse 3). After scrolling through the *Interlinear*, write down what it means:

_____

_____

_____

_____

Though no one is 100 percent sure what *selah* means, writers likely meant it as a pause. Unlike our modern musical symbols for *rest*, a *selah* isn't for a certain amount of time. The person conducting senses this sort of pause and leads according to how long they feel the pause needs to take.

4. What do you think we're getting at here? How would a *pause* and God being a *rock* correspond? Why might this be important?

_____

_____

_____

5. What could you do to invoke *selah* into your daily life? How might this help mature your relationship with Christ?

_____

_____

_____

_____

Perhaps David's secondary purpose in using this word was to remind first himself, then the entire nation of Israel, to rest, pausing in the strength of the Lord. When we find ourselves in the darkness, we don't have to live in panic and exhaustion. Instead, we can reflect and bask in God's security and refuge.

Spend some time reflecting on this quote by Mother Teresa, asking God to meet you in rest and strength:

In the silence of the heart God speaks. If you face God in prayer and silence, God will speak to you. Then you will know that you are nothing. It is only when you realize your nothingness, your emptiness, that God can fill you with Himself. Souls of prayer are souls of great silence.[4]

Heavenly Father,

Amen.

WEEK 7 • *Day 3*

 READ PSALM 18:4-18

Today we're going to get into all sorts of imagery as David describes God's protection and deliverance. This isn't just wishful thinking—remember, David is looking back over his life. He's talking about things he actually experienced, the firm reality that God has protected and delivered him time and time again. Life with God means that each of us can find strength in our struggles by reminding ourselves of God's faithfulness in the past.

1. Go through the passage here, underlining words or phrases that show David's distress and circling those that talk about God's hand of aid.

4-5 For when the ropes of death wrapped around me
and terrifying torrents of destruction overwhelmed me,
taking me to death's door, to doom's domain,
6 I cried out to you in my distress, the delivering God,
and from your temple-throne you heard my troubled cry.
My sobs came right into your heart
and you turned your face to rescue me.
7 The earth itself shivered and shook.
It reeled and rocked before him.
As the mountains trembled, they melted away!
For his anger was kindled, burning on my behalf.
8 Fierce flames leapt from his mouth,
erupting with blazing, burning coals as smoke
and fire encircled him.
9-10 He stretched heaven's curtain open and came to my defense.
Swiftly he rode to earth as the stormy sky was lowered.

He rode a chariot of thunderclouds amidst thick darkness,
a cherub his steed as he swooped down,
soaring on the wings of Spirit-wind.
¹¹ Wrapped and hidden in the thick-cloud darkness,
his thunder-tabernacle surrounded him.
He hid himself in mystery-darkness;
the dense rain clouds were his garments.
¹² Suddenly the brilliance of his presence broke through
with lightning bolts and with a mighty storm from heaven—
like a tempest dropping coals of fire.
¹³ The Lord thundered, the great God above every god
spoke with his thunder-voice from the skies.
What fearsome hailstones and flashes of fire were before him!
¹⁴ He released his lightning-arrows, and routed my foes.
See how they ran and scattered in fear!
¹⁵ Then with his mighty roar he laid bare the foundations of
the earth,
uncovering the secret source of the sea.
The hidden depths of land and sea were exposed
by the hurricane-blast of his hot breath.
¹⁶ He then reached down from heaven,
all the way from the sky to the sea.
He reached down into my darkness to rescue me!
He took me out of my calamity and chaos
and drew me to himself,
taking me from the depths of my despair!
¹⁷ Even though I was helpless in the hands
of my hateful, strong enemy,
you were good to deliver me.
¹⁸ When I was at my weakest, my enemies attacked—
but the Lord held on to me.

PSALM 18:4-18, TPT

2. What was your favorite verse, phrase, or imagery in this passage? Why?

_____

_____

_____

The portion that jumped out at me most is verse 6:

I cried out to you in my distress, the delivering God,
and from your temple-throne you heard my troubled cry.
My sobs came right into your heart
and you turned your face to rescue me.

3. Please head to the BLB, click on verse 6 and then *Interlinear*. Tap on the phrase *I called* or *qara'* (קָרָא, pronounced *kah-rah*) in Hebrew. Write some of the synonyms below:

_____

_____

David is saying he cries out to God in prayer—but did you notice he doesn't list a memorized set of words? He doesn't say, "When I uttered this litany or repetition of words, God heard me and helped me out." Neither did he say, "Only when I expressed the most beautifully eloquent prayer, my heavenly Father's ear turned toward me, and He came to my aid."

As we learned in our word study, *qara'* (קָרָא) means "to call, cry, utter a loud sound."[5] Did you catch that last one? A loud *sound* . . . not even necessarily a coherent word. So often we think our prayers need to be neat and tidy, wrapped with a beautifully crisp bow. Whether we do it to show the world we are good Christians or because we're convinced that the Lord listens because we speak in such beautiful prose, we're massively missing the boat. Prayer isn't about eloquence at all.

Prayer can be prewritten, beautifully expressed and presented to the Lord, sure. But it can also be falling on our face, dirty, disheveled, not knowing how to even form a coherent sentence. Our prayers may be eloquent one moment and a battle cry the next. We can be tongue-tied, unintelligible, muffled, stammering, and even wordless.

Romans 8:26-27 (ESV) helps us understand how this works:

> Likewise the Spirit helps us in our weakness. For we do not know what to pray for as we ought, but the Spirit himself intercedes for us with groanings too deep for words. And he who searches hearts knows what is the mind of the Spirit, because the Spirit intercedes for the saints according to the will of God.

4. What does *intercession* (or *interceding*) mean? (Feel free to look it up if you don't know.)

One night, after a special event at the Christian college I went to, a guy came up to me as my friends and I were heading back to our dorm. He said, "I'm interceding for you." I looked at him like he was a crazy person, said, "Uhhhh . . . thanks," and kept walking. I had no clue what he was talking about or how to respond. Was this how "super spiritual" guys flirted and tried to hit on girls? Or was he serious? I was so confused that I pulled out my dictionary when I got back to my room (yes, this was before Google).

The dictionary basically taught me that this term was all about *pleading, advocating,* and *meditating on the behalf of someone else.*

And what we learn in Romans 8 is that, unlike this guy who didn't know me and what my needs were, the Holy Spirit does and can translate the deepest ugly-cry prayers or wide-eyed *I don't even know where to start, what to say, or what to pray about this* thoughts into powerful and articulate requests and conversations with our heavenly Father.

Our gut-cry prayers are heard and understood more than we even understand them—because the Holy Spirit translates our hearts and presents them to God Himself. Isn't that amazing?

I love praying and have most certainly felt the impact of coming before God no matter how simple my words, but I sometimes wish I was one of those women who prays and makes everyone think, *Wow. God definitely heard that one—it was absolutely incredible!* Is that silly to admit? I'm sure you've heard those people—where they pray and you feel ready to jump into anything because their words were so full of life, inspiring beyond measure!

5. Do you sometimes feel intimidated about praying? If so, why?

I love praying by myself throughout the day but it's taken years for me to be comfortable praying in front of others. If you want complete honesty, I still struggle with confidence doing so because I often don't feel like my prayers are enough. Deep enough, prettily worded enough, bold and impactful enough. And that's such a lie right from the evil one himself. Truly. God listens to the heart behind our prayers more than the words we use.

6. As David continues on past verse 6 and talks about what happens after his prayer reached God's ears, what happens? (Hint: Look at Psalm 18:7.)

7. Why is God angry in this verse?

We are God's precious children. Because of His deep love for His child, God's anger burns bright when David is despised, harmed, and suffering because of someone else.

8. How would you describe God here? Go back and look over the imagery that David uses in this passage. What words come to mind when you read about the shaking earth, fire blazing from God's mouth, garments made of dense rain clouds, and the like?

Our God is wild, strong, and protective. He gets angry when we are mistreated and harmed. There's no evidence that David ever saw any of this with his own eyes, but instead he is using beautiful symbolism that connects back to Moses' encounter with God at Mount Sinai.

¹⁶ On the morning of the third day there were thunders and lightnings and a thick cloud on the mountain and a very loud trumpet blast, so that all the people in the camp trembled. ¹⁷ Then Moses brought the people out of the camp to meet God, and they took their stand at the foot of the mountain. ¹⁸ Now Mount Sinai was wrapped in smoke because the LORD had descended on it in fire. The smoke of it went up like the smoke of a kiln, and the whole mountain trembled greatly. ¹⁹ And as the sound of the trumpet grew louder and louder, Moses spoke, and God answered him in thunder. ²⁰ The LORD came down on Mount Sinai, to the top of the mountain. And the LORD called Moses to the top of the mountain, and Moses went up.

EXODUS 19:16-20, ESV

9. What similarities do you see between David's words and this scene? Write the words or phrases below:

_____

_____

_____

Our God is powerful and He loves you. Deeply. He doesn't just sit on His throne in heaven, watching things unfold on earth below Him. He is a profoundly personal God, involved and active in our lives. His hand is on us, and He walks beside us. Yes, we'll go through hard stuff. Yes, there will be times we can't figure out why He didn't stop something from happening. Things may not be perfect and seamless in your life right now, but *He* is perfect and seamless, and He has a grand purpose: deep growth out of the ground of this hard stuff. God's end goal is more beautiful than you could ever imagine. And we'll never, ever be alone in it. In fact, He promises to be with us forever.

Jesus, undeterred, went right ahead and gave his charge: "God authorized and commanded me to commission you: Go out and train everyone you meet, far and near, in this way of life, marking them by baptism in the threefold name: Father, Son, and Holy Spirit. Then instruct them in the practice of all I have commanded you. I'll be with you as you do this, day after day after day, right up to the end of the age."

MATTHEW 28:18-20

 Let's end today in prayer as we thank the Lord for His never-ending presence in our lives, no matter what season, struggle, or success.

Amen.

WEEK 7 • *Day 4*

 READ PSALM 18:16-24

Like David, I've had to battle to surrender all of my broken pieces to God. As I do, though, I am reminded that God never does anything halfway. If He offers rescue, He will ultimately rescue us completely.

If He offers healing, He will eventually heal us fully. His redemption has no caveats.

David goes on to say, "He rescued me from my strong enemy and from those who hated me, for they were too mighty for me. They confronted me in the day of my calamity, but the LORD was my support. He brought me out into a broad place; he rescued me, because he delighted in me" (Psalm 18:17-19, ESV).

1. What does David mean by "He brought me out into a broad place"? Go ahead and look it up in the *Interlinear* and share your thoughts below:

2. That wasn't super helpful, was it? Let's dig a little deeper. Head right on over to the *Text Commentaries* to see what you can make of this phrase we're curious about:

In the footnotes, the study portion of my ESV Bible says that David talks about his enemies as "swirling waters about to drown him" (Psalm 18:16-19), and God rescuing him and "set[ting] him on a **broad place**, ground that is high and dry" (Psalm 18:19).[6] Matthew Henry says, "There were waters deep and many, waters out of which he was to be drawn. . . . But, in the midst of his troubles, the Lord was his stay, so that he did not sink."[7] And God offers us the same rescue: "He brought me forth also out of my straits into a large place, where I had room, not only to turn but to thrive in."[8] That is certainly a description of being "brought out into a broad place" that makes sense to me!

3. Read Matthew Henry's explanation again and then sketch something that helps you visualize what he's saying. (And if you're not much of an artist, don't worry! This is just to help you picture it—a stick-figure drawing is fine!)

Spurgeon also explains this phrase:

Sweet is pleasure after pain. Enlargement is the more delightful after a season of pinching poverty and sorrowful confinement. . . . The Lord does not leave his work half done, for having routed the foe he leads out the captive into liberty. Large indeed is the possession and place of the believer in Jesus, there need be no limit to his peace, for there is no bound to his privilege.[9]

God longs to take you out of dangerous waters and set you in a place you can thrive in. His rescue is also for you.

4. Take a moment to rewrite the comments from Henry and Spurgeon into your own words.

Isn't it amazing how much more we get out of the Bible when we dig in and do more than simply scan the words? Reading the Bible can grow our understanding of who God is, but digging into the Scriptures will transform us.

Okay, let's keep going and look into Psalm 18:20-24 (ESV):

20 The LORD dealt with me according to my righteousness;
    according to the cleanness of my hands he rewarded me.
21 For I have kept the ways of the LORD,
    and have not wickedly departed from my God.
22 For all his rules were before me,
    and his statutes I did not put away from me.
23 I was blameless before him,
    and I kept myself from my guilt.
24 So the LORD has rewarded me according to my righteousness,
    according to the cleanness of my hands in his sight.

5. Underline or highlight verses 20 and 24. Does anything strike you as strange sounding about these verses? If so, what?

In both verses, David talks about the cleanness of his hands. Really, David? After last week's look at Bathsheba and the murder of her husband Uriah in 2 Samuel 11, I certainly wouldn't say David walks around in righteousness with perfectly clean hands.

Let's read this same passage in *The Message*:

> GOD made my life complete
> when I placed all the pieces before him.
> When I got my act together,
> he gave me a fresh start.
> Now I'm alert to GOD's ways;
> I don't take God for granted.
> Every day I review the ways he works;
> I try not to miss a trick.
> I feel put back together,
> and I'm watching my step.
> GOD rewrote the text of my life
> when I opened the book of my heart to his eyes.
>
> PSALM 18:20-24

6. Wow; okay . . . that makes more sense, right? David isn't being snobbish and uppity, acting like he's truly blameless, guiltless, and pure in all he does. What is he actually saying?

David is admitting that there were times in his life where he tried to do things himself. We've certainly seen this throughout our study together! But he's also acknowledging that "GOD made [his] life complete when [he] placed all the pieces before him" (Psalm 18:20).

We can get so busy thinking we can do things on our own that we sometimes forget to ask for God's opinion and guidance. We need to kneel before Him, spreading out all the pieces, lifting our hands in surrender, saying, "Here! Take it! This is yours. All of it. Do with it as You please, and use me for Your greatest purpose."

"When I got my act together, he gave me a fresh start" (Psalm 18:20) isn't telling us that we need to become sinless to be accepted by God. David isn't saying he's perfect and amazing, and he's certainly not intending a self-righteous tone of arrogance. Instead, David is pointing to the unfathomable grace of God: *Yes, I messed up, and I continue to mess up—but God wipes it all clean. I strive to live according to God's desires for me, and even when I miss the mark, He loves me and forgives me. When I humbled myself, knowing that it's only in Him I can do things, I got a fresh start.*

David is not denying his own fallenness but celebrating the incredible work of the Holy Spirit. As Spurgeon notes,

> Is he to deny his own consciousness, and to despise the work of the Holy Ghost, by hypocritically making himself out to be worse than he is? A godly man prizes his integrity very highly, or else he would not be a godly man at all; is he to be called proud because he will not readily lose the jewel of a reputable character?[10]

Like David, I've had to battle to surrender all of my broken pieces to God. When I did, though, "GOD rewrote the text of my life when I opened the book of my heart to his eyes" (Psalm 18:24). I'm so grateful to God for my fresh start. Aren't you?

7. How would you explain Psalm 18:20-24? Write it out in your own words and reflect on how it could apply to you:

As we continue reading Psalm 18, David celebrates God's mercy and forgiveness. The ESV translates Psalm 18:25-26 as

> 25 With the merciful you show yourself merciful;
>   with the blameless man you show yourself blameless;
> 26 with the purified you show yourself pure.

Throughout the Bible, we can see the powerful truth of the grace David's talking about, and when I read these words about being purified, I immediately think about a passage in Isaiah.

8. Flip to Isaiah 1:18 and write it here:

9. What does Isaiah 1:18 have to do with Psalm 18:20-26?

In the sight of the Lord, we are clean and forgiven. Sinless—"white as snow." Psalm 103:12 (ESV) hammers this home:

> As far as the east is from the west,
>   so far does he remove our transgressions from us.

Transgressions, or *pesha'* (פֶּשַׁע, pronounced *peh-shah*), means "rebellion" and "sin."[11] The thing with transgressions is that they're often accompanied by shame and humiliation. When my kids get caught doing something they shouldn't, they hang their head and have a hard time making eye contact. We're often the same with God. Even after asking His forgiveness, we look down at ourselves instead of up at Him.

But the rest of that passage in Psalm 103 tells us how God meets us in this:

> [10] He does not deal with us according to our sins,
>   nor repay us according to our iniquities.
> [11] For as high as the heavens are above the earth,
>   so great is his steadfast love toward those who fear him;
> [12] as far as the east is from the west,
>   so far does he remove our transgressions from us.
> [13] As a father shows compassion to his children,
>   so the LORD shows compassion to those who fear him.
> PSLAM 103:10-13, ESV

That's what's so incredible about grace. We don't deserve it; we aren't worthy of it. We don't have the right to it. And yet the Lord gives it freely because He loves us more than we could ever wrap our minds around. David did his best to write about this love, but even in his eloquent prose, he only pricked at God's magnificence. Someday we'll understand it completely when we stand before Him in heaven. But today, we can only open our hands and say, "Yes, Lord.

Forgive me for my past. Send me out to do Your good work. And use me until there is nothing left to use."

 Spend some time with God, reflecting on His love and grace in your life:

_____

_____

_____

_____

_____

_____

_____

_____

_____

Amen.

WEEK 7 • *Day 5*

READ PSALM 18:25-36

This is our last day together. Craziness! And truth be told, I'm a little blue about reaching the end with you because I hate endings. But here's what I know: If you've reached this far, it's because you're a bold woman who loves Jesus. You've dug in to learn more about God and His glory, and because of that, I know this isn't *actually* the end. You may still like to use a prewritten study (which is great!), but you no longer *need* one because you know how to break apart Scripture yourself. You know how to search up the Hebrew and dive into commentaries. You know how to wrestle with God for the deeper meaning of His Word and how it applies to your life.

It's truly been an honor to walk with you as we've figured out how to say yes to God even when things are hard and dark. Yes, you may struggle to keep saying yes to Him. You might feel like it's easier to simply walk away, or like all you want to do is curl up in the fetal position and never leave. I get it. I don't talk about it often, but I've actually been at the place where I thought it would be easier to just end my life because the emotional pain was too severe. David gets that place too. Life is hard and full of struggle. But it's how we continue getting up and saying yes that matters most.

When we say yes to God in the darkness, we acknowledge that this pain is not the end. It might feel like this darkness will go on forever. We may feel stuck, like this will be the reality for the rest of our days. But that's a lie. If we follow Jesus, darkness is never the end. Jesus Christ *is* light, and "in him is no darkness at all" (1 John 1:5, ESV). The closer we get to Him and the longer we stay by His side, the more light He'll help us see in our dark places. And eventually? Eventually that darkness will be nothing but fleeting shadow. The light has already won (Romans 8:38-39; Colossians 1:13).

Today we'll dig in as we always do, but I'm leaving some of Psalm 18 unstudied because I want you to continue on and delve in yourself tomorrow, or the next day. Or the day after that. Inquire, unearth, and sift through David's words. We dived into most of the psalms that correspond with 1 and 2 Samuel stories, but there is still so much more of David's life that we have yet to turn inside out:

- his life as a successful warrior before becoming a fugitive;
- more hardship while running from the crazed king;
- the death of both Jonathan and Saul;
- how David met his wives and why he married them;
- the drama that unfolded with his many children;
- his eldest son Absalom attempting to take control of the kingship and all of Nathan's words in 2 Samuel 12 coming true;
- and so much more!

I encourage you to go down rabbit holes and dive into the chapters we didn't cover here because there's so much more to learn, so much more to discover.

Okay, with all that said . . . let's open our Bibles to Psalm 18.

1. Flip back to days 1 through 3 of this week and write a quick synopsis of what's going on:

_____

_____

_____

_____

_____

Do you remember last week's story about the man who had always thought that God was yelling at him through the Ten Commandments? And how God reframed those commandments through the lens of His kindness and love? It is with that same spirit that this portion of Psalm 18 was written.

Let's read Psalm 18:25-36 together. As you do, circle all the things God *is* in one color and what He *does* in another.

> ²⁵ You are loyal to those who are loyal;
>   with the innocent, You prove to be innocent;
> ²⁶ With the clean, You prove to be clean;
>   and with the twisted, You make Yourself contrary.
> ²⁷ For You rescue humble people,
>   but You bring the proud back in line.
> ²⁸ You are the lamp who lights my way;
>   the Eternal, my God, lights up my darkness.
> ²⁹ With Your help, I can conquer an army;
>   I can leap over walls with a helping hand from You.

³⁰ Everything God does is perfect;
    the promise of the Eternal rings true;
    He stands as a shield for all who hide in Him.
³¹ Who is the True God except the Eternal?
    Who stands like a rock except our God?
³² The True God who encircled me with strength
    and made my pathway straight.
³³ He made me sure-footed as a deer
    and placed me high up where I am safe.
³⁴ He teaches me to fight
    so that my arms can bend a bronze bow.
³⁵ You have shielded me with Your salvation,
    supporting me with Your strong right hand,
    and it makes me strong.
³⁶ You taught me how to walk with care
    so my feet will not slip.

PSALM 18:25-36, VOICE

We know that God did great things in David's lifetime and protected him in many ways. But even when He allowed David to struggle and go through difficulty, God's character always remained the same, and the same is true today. For example, He is loyal (Psalm 18:25) and He is perfect (Psalm 18:30). These things are not circumstantial but are characteristics of God's very being.

David's responses to God's actions and character (*what He does* and *who He is*) are thanksgiving and adoration. Did you know that there is a difference between these two things?

2. What do you think the difference is?

Thankfulness is being grateful for *what God has done*, whereas adoration is being grateful *for who God is*. And what God *does* emerges out of who God *is*.

3. Look at the first line of verse 28. When you read the words "You are the lamp who lights my way," what do you learn about who God is?

   God is _____

The Old and New Testaments are tied together with the thread of learning *who God is*. Let's quickly flip over to the first chapter of 1 John to shed more light on this topic (horrible pun totally intended). *The Message* translates 1 John 1:5 as

This, in essence, is the message we heard from Christ and are passing on to you: God is light, pure light; there's not a trace of darkness in him.

4. Okay—so if God *is* light, what does He *do* for us? (Hint: Head back to Psalm 18:28 and read the rest of that verse.)

5. He "lights up my darkness." So, what exactly *is* darkness? Let's head to the BLB and look up this word in the *Interlinear*. What words further illuminate the meaning? (I can't stop the puns!)

"Obscurity," "secret place," "misery," "destruction," "sorrow," and "wickedness."[12] I've most certainly been in this kind of darkness, and I have a feeling you have too. I love how it says a "secret place," because that's how it feels, doesn't it? Like we need to keep it down deep and not share it with anyone.

The lexicon compares darkness to a underground prison and lists Isaiah 42:7 next to that definition. In that passage, we once again find Jesus and the character of God Himself woven from the Old Testament into the New. As Isaiah's prophecies share about the coming Messiah, God says this:

> [6] I am the LORD; I have called **you** in righteousness;
>   I will take **you** by the hand and keep **you**;
> I will give **you** as a covenant for the people,
>   a light for the nations,
>   [7] to open the eyes that are blind,
> to bring out the prisoners from the dungeon,
>   from the prison those who sit in darkness.
>
> ISAIAH 42:6-7, ESV, EMPHASIS MINE

See the words I made bold? Each of the times God uses the word **you** here, He does so in a singular way.

7. What do you think is going on here? Who is the **you** that God is speaking to?

God isn't spouting a blanket *you*—He's talking to Jesus. Jesus is who brings the prisoners out of the darkness. With His power and through the Holy Spirit, our eyes are opened to His love and we can be brought out from the darkness we feel trapped in. Jesus Himself confirms this in John 8:12 (ESV):

Again Jesus spoke to them, saying, "I am the light of the world. Whoever follows me will not walk in darkness, but will have the light of life."

8. Head to the BLB and use the *Interlinear* and/or the *Commentaries* to delve in more to this verse. What does Jesus mean when He says we "will not walk in darkness"?

_____

_____

_____

Jesus isn't saying we will never encounter difficulty or wade through dark times. What He is promising, though, is we're not stuck in darkness. Depression, anxiety, fear, sin, and living in a secret place aren't foregone conclusions. They aren't forever. Now, in no way am I saying not to take your anxiety medication or stray away from what your doctor has told you to do. Sometimes depression and anxiety are clinical, and God can reveal His work through medications and therapy alongside prayer and Scripture. What I am saying, though, is that we often wade through unnecessary difficulty because we're not walking in alignment with Him. He alone is the Light in the midst of all our darkness.

We can dig a little bit more into this idea of light in Psalm 119:

129 Your decrees inspire wonder;
    because of that, my soul desires to keep them.
130 **When Your words are unveiled, light shines forth;**
    they bring understanding to the simple.
131 My desire for Your commands
    left me waiting, open-mouthed and panting.
132 Acknowledge me and show me Your grace
    as is Your habit toward all those who love Your name.

¹³³ Guide my steps in the ways of Your word,
    and do not let any sin control me.
¹³⁴ Rescue me from the torment of my human oppressors
    so that I may live according Your decrees.
¹³⁵ Let Your face shine upon Your servant,
    and help me to learn what You require.
¹³⁶ My eyes shed rivers of tears
    whenever people fail to keep Your teaching.

PSALM 119:129-136, VOICE, EMPHASIS MINE

9. We see the reference to the light again in verse 130, but let's also take a look at verse 131. How could this verse help us walk in "the light of life" (John 8:12, ESV)?

We need to pray for the desire to walk closely with Christ. We need to pray for a deep thirst and hunger for Him. Several years ago, when I struggled to pray on a consistent basis, I prayed for the *desire* to pray. And you know what? God gave it to me.

I know there are days when pulling out your Bible and sitting down with it feels more like homework than *I-can't-wait-to-do-it* work, so ask God to put that desire into your heart. Ask Him to give you a voracious hunger for spending time with Him and in His Word. If you continued to ask the Lord for something like this, why on earth would He refuse to give it to you? (*Spoiler alert: He'll* absolutely *give you this desire if you ask Him to and continue spending time with Him, even on days you'd rather do something else.*)

This week, we've seen a lot of imagery that helps us understand God in a deeper way. As we return to Psalm 18, we're brought back to many of the things we've already read about who God *is* and what He *does*:

³¹ For who is God, but the LORD?
  And who is a rock, except our God?—
³² the God who equipped me with strength
  and made my way blameless.
³³ He made my feet like the feet of a deer
  and set me secure on the heights.

PSALM 18:31-33, ESV

Earlier this week, we learned about God being our Rock (or rrrrrr-rock, as my Ethiopian son says in his accented English), and we've learned how God's forgiveness makes us blameless and turns our hands clean, no matter how dirty with sin they've become. We dug into what it meant when David said he was taken out of the waters and set on a high place so he could thrive. All these things are mentioned again here in verses 31-33 (above).

10. Why do you think that is? (Hint: Look at verse 32.)

It's because God equipped David with strength—strength to not give up when times were far from easy, strength to trust Him, strength to want to walk in the light. And strength to continue in relationship with his heavenly Father, even when things weren't going as he wanted them to.

God had a plan for David. And like our lives, it wasn't a straight path from *a* to *b* or from *b* to *c*. But think about this: David was anointed for something. Samuel may have known it was kingship, but nothing in the Bible tells us that the prophet shared that news with David. He knew he was set apart, but for what exactly, he wasn't sure. There had only been one king before him, so protocol was not set yet.

But God brought David into King Saul's life in several ways:

a. *as a harp player*—By God placing David in this role, he could peer into Saul's private life. It was here that David saw what home life looked like for the king as David observed Saul and his family on a personal level;

b. *as an armor bearer*—What other job could have prepared David in the way this position did? Because David oversaw Saul's armor, he was required to be with Saul at all times during war, just waiting for the king to put it all on and wage battle with his men. Because David was basically a fly on the wall, he was privy to conversations and strategy between Saul and his generals. He saw what worked and what was unsuccessful. David could observe the king's interactions with military leaders and how he responded in success and in failure; and

c. *as a fugitive*—Even in the years David struggled living on the run from Saul, God used for it His ultimate glory. It was during this time of seeming darkness that David's faith in his heavenly Father grew. It was here David realized he could do nothing apart from God and that he needed Him more than anything else.

As we wrap up together, I want you to reflect on something: *What experiences have helped build you into the strong woman you are today?* Hindsight is always 20/20, so walk through your experiences, both good and hard. Talk with the Lord about these things. David could never have been the man he was without the struggles and without first being a harpist and an armor bearer. Things that might have seemed obscure and unrelated actually had deep purpose, giving David the experience needed for the future.

³ We also celebrate in seasons of suffering because we know that when we suffer we develop endurance, ⁴ which shapes our characters. When our characters are refined, we learn what it means to hope and anticipate God's goodness.
ROMANS 5:3-4, VOICE

A life of ease rarely produces tenacity and substance. Be that woman of substance . . . and know that nothing is wasted. Keep saying *yes* to Him in the darkness. Because remember, beautiful people don't just happen. We become who we are through the choices we make to move forward in the middle of our hardest stories. Our wounds are not our worth, but what we do in the middle of our pain matters. Not saying yes might feel safe (because we'll remain right where we are), but saying yes could completely change the trajectory of our entire lives. I would rather risk saying yes than live a life of regret, wondering what would have happened if I had trusted God in the darkness.

Remember, God is light, and in Him there is no darkness at all (1 John 1:5). From the creation of the world, to the defeat of sin, to the hardest parts of our very own stories—He is always, *always* bringing light out of the darkness.

Dear Lord Jesus, as strange as it sounds, thank You for struggle. Thank You that I'm beginning to understand that with You at the helm, difficulty can develop me into a woman of strength and endurance as my character is shaped. Please grow me in a way that I crave relationship with You and cling tighter to You. Teach me through the darkness and bring light to it, Father, because it's painful and just so very messy . . .

Your daughter, forever and ever. Amen.

WEEK 7 *Notes*

Share your biggest takeaways from this week:

Acknowledgments

Jesus: You're funny. I never, ever would have thought I'd write Bible studies. But the other day when I asked You, "Why did I waste so much time on an art history degree if that wasn't even the plan?"—remember what you whispered to my heart? *Nothing is wasted. You now study the Bible exactly the way you learned to study art—digging into culture, society, politics, and everything in between—except now you're doing it to figure out what inspired Me to include each story, parable, psalm, person, or tiniest little detail.*

No experience is ever wasted. I pray, Lord Jesus, that none of me is wasted either.

Benny: Thank you for helping push me out of bed each morning so I have time to write, study, and spend time with Jesus before the kids wake. Thank you for taking them on fun "daddy dates" on some evenings and weekends so I can do that some more. Thank you for being my sounding board, my encourager when I thought, *Who am I to do this?*, and the love of my life. I am so overwhelmingly in love with you.

Momma and Daddy: Thank you for creating a home in which I saw both of you read and study Scripture. Daddy, you and your color-coded, highlighted pages—and Momma, you at the dining table, workbooks and Bible spread in front of you on warm days . . . and on the floor next to the heating vent when it was cold. Thank you for being living examples to me.

Elsabet, Imani, Laith, Anton, Ezekiel, and Abreham: I have no idea if you'll ever sit down and do the studies I write, but I do pray that Jesus captivates you the same way He does me. I pray that seeing me constantly pour over Scripture lights a fire in you, too. Loves, *dive in.* Don't live on what others regurgitate to you about God's Word . . . figure it out yourself. See and learn about Jesus yourself. If you ever don't know where to start, ask Jesus. He'll teach you. He is, after all, the original Teacher. I love every one of you and am so proud to be your mom. XO

Kiesha Yokers: Thank you for loving and encouraging me well. I've never met anyone who makes me laugh harder and yet challenges and encourages me so deeply. I love you, girl.

Nirup Alphonse: This is all your fault. Thank you for . . . *challenging me?*

telling me? ordering me? to stop leading Bible studies that I've purchased and instead write them myself. Thank you for telling me I really could do this. Thanks for believing in me, dear friend.

Jana Burson: Thank you for taking a chance on me in so many ways. And thank you for being the type of agent who isn't just about business but loves on me well. You're amazing.

Don Pape: I'm still pinching myself that you believed in me enough to sign me for three studies. Not only that, but for standing with me while sharing that we need to "skate to where the puck is going to be, not where it has been" (Wayne Gretzky). You're a true visionary. Thank you for your emails and texts saying you're praying for me and for taking us all out to fun dinners because I'm not just your author, I'm family.

Caitlyn Carlson: Who'd have known a cup of coffee to talk about my proposal would lead to acquiring not only three books but also a deep friendship?! The BEST. Thank you for both pushing and having grace with me as you edited my one billion words. I adore you, girl.

Elizabeth Schroll, Olivia Eldredge, and Dave Zimmerman: Thank you for sharing your editorial giftings, your granola bars, your dried mango, and your jumper cables. You are amazing friends and fantastic talents. Thanks for loving me well. (PS—When can we go back to that Thai place?)

David Geeslin, Madeline Daniels, Isabella Cortes, Linda Schmitt, Adam Graber, and Libby Dykstra: I'm overwhelmed to have not only the incredible team over at NavPress but you at Tyndale, too. You, dear friends, heard me. I had a vision and you caught my excitement, even though it's not necessarily "the way things are done." Thank you for jumping in and sharing the message of Jesus in the way I felt Him asking me to. I've enjoyed every second.

Creighton Petro: I love that one day I'm walking into Chauncy's office, meeting her for the first time, and the next day she tells me, "You have to meet my husband." (Chauncy, you were SO right.) Thank you for believing in me enough to jump on board with *Let's Party Like Girls* first and now all the video fun for our Get Wisdom series. I hope this is just the beginning!

Hannah Brencher: Sweet friend, little did I know several years ago while reading *Come Matter Here* that one of its chapters would inspire the title of this book. In fact, your last line in chapter 6 says: "What is good enough, real enough, strong enough for us that, when everything else fails us, we will still say yes in the dark?" Right there in the margin, I wrote the words: *My next book title?* Proud of you and your vulnerability. Thank you for all you do and are. XO

Appendix

If you're new to Bible commentaries or want to expand your reference library, I recommend the following options.

GENERAL BIBLE COMMENTARIES

FULL BIBLE

Henry, Matthew. *Matthew Henry's Concise Commentary of the Whole Bible*. Nashville: Thomas Nelson, 2003.

Wenham, G. J. et al., eds. *New Bible Commentary*, 21st-century ed. Downers Grove, IL: InterVarsity Press, 1994.

OLD TESTAMENT

Goldstein, Elyse, ed. *The Women's Torah Commentary: New Insights from Women Rabbis on the 54 Weekly Torah Portions*. Woodstock, VT: Jewish Lights, 2000.

Walton, John H., Victor H. Matthews, and Mark W. Chavalas. *IVP Bible Background Commentary: Old Testament*. Downers Grove, IL: IVP Academic, 2000.

NEW TESTAMENT

Keener, Craig S. *IVP Bible Background Commentary: New Testament*. Downers Grove, IL: IVP Academic, 2014.

COMMENTARIES ON PSALMS

Arnold, Bill T. *1 & 2 Samuel: The NIV Application Commentary*. Grand Rapids, MI: Zondervan, 2003.

Baldwin, Joyce G. *1 and 2 Samuel*. Tyndale Old Testament Commentaries. Downers Grove, IL: InterVarsity Press, 2008.

Kelly, Ryan. *1–2 Samuel: A 12-Week Study*. Wheaton, IL: Crossway, 2018.

Longman, Tremper, III. *Psalms*. Tyndale Old Testament Commentaries (Downers Grove, IL: InterVarsity Press, 2014).

Wilcock, Michael. *The Message of Psalms 1–72: Songs for the People of God*, The Bible
　　Speaks Today. Downers Grove, IL: InterVarsity Press, 2001.
Wilcock, Michael. *The Message of Psalms 73–150: Songs for the People of God*, The Bible
　　Speaks Today. Downers Grove, IL: InterVarsity Press, 2001.

ADDITIONAL RESOURCES

APPS

Bible Gateway (or biblegateway.com)
Bible Hub (or biblehub.com)
Bible Study Tools (or biblestudytools.com)
Blue Letter Bible (or blueletterbible.org)
YouVersion (or youversion.com)

BIBLE DICTIONARY

Marshall, I. Howard, et al., eds. *New Bible Dictionary*. 3rd ed. Leicester, England:
　　InterVarsity Press, 2004.

BIBLICAL HISTORY

Bright, John. *A History of Israel*. 4th ed. Louisville, KY: Westminster John Knox, 2000.

BIBLICAL MAPS

Isbouts, Jean-Pierre. *The Biblical World: An Illustrated Atlas*. Washington, DC: National
　　Geographic, 2007.
Rose Book of Bible Charts, Maps, and Time Lines. Torrance, CA: Rose Publishing, 2015.

Notes

INTRODUCTION
1. Please see the appendix.

WEEK 1: WHEN DARKNESS SETS IN
1. C. H. Spurgeon, "Psalm 59," accessed November 22, 2019, https://www
.blueletterbible.org/Comm/spurgeon_charles/tod/ps059.cfm?a=255011.
2. Blue Letter Bible, "Lexicon: Strong's H4397, *mal'ak*," accessed November 22, 2019,
https://www.blueletterbible.org/lang/lexicon/lexicon.cfm?Strongs=H4397&t=ESV.
3. Charles Spurgeon, *Lectures to My Students: Complete and Unabridged* (Grand Rapids,
MI: Zondervan, 2010), 37.
4. Beth Moore, *David: Seeking a Heart Like His* (Nashville, TN: LifeWay, 2010), 40.
5. NIV, NIVUK.
6. Blue Letter Bible, "Lexicon: Strong's H157—*'ahab*," accessed November 22, 2019,
https://www.blueletterbible.org/lang/lexicon/lexicon.cfm?Strongs=H157&t=ESV.

WEEK 2: RESPONDING IN THE DARKNESS
1. J. R. R. Tolkien, *The Lord of the Rings* (Boston: Houghton Mifflin, 2004), 170.
2. Matthew Henry, *Commentary on the Whole Bible*, one vol. ed. (Grand Rapids, MI:
Zondervan, 1960), 230.
3. C. S. Lewis, *The Problem of Pain* (New York: HarperCollins, 2001), 91.
4. Teresa Swanstrom Anderson, *Beautifully Interrupted: When God Holds the Pen That
Writes Your Story* (Franklin, TN: Worthy Books, 2018).
5. Neil Howe, "Millennials and the Loneliness Epidemic," *Forbes*, May 3, 2019,
https://www.forbes.com/sites/neilhowe/2019/05/03/millennials-and-the-loneliness
-epidemic/#68597cf77676.

WEEK 3: FINDING GOD IN THE DARKNESS
1. Dictionary.com, s.v. "sinner (*n.*)," accessed November 24, 2019,
https://www.dictionary.com/browse/sinner?s=t.
2. Dictionary.com, s.v. "transgress (*v.*)," accessed November 24, 2019,
https://www.dictionary.com/browse/transgressor?s=t.

3. Blue Letter Bible, "Lexicon: Strong's H8085—*shama'*," accessed December 3, 2019, https://www.blueletterbible.org/lang/lexicon/lexicon.cfm?Strongs=H8085&t=ESV.

4. Author's paraphrase.

5. Max Lucado, *Is God Good?* (Wheaton, IL: Good News Publishers, 2014), accessed January 10, 2020, https://www.crossway.org/tracts/is-god-good-3580/.

6. This saying is frequently quoted (and frequently misattributed). According to Quote Investigator, Charles Eads first said these words, in a 1959 lecture; see https://quoteinvestigator.com/2019/09/15/hurt/.

7. Blue Letter Bible, "Lexicon: H3117—*yowm*," accessed November 24, 2019, https://www.blueletterbible.org/lang/lexicon/lexicon.cfm?Strongs=H3117&t=ESV.

8. Blue Letter Bible, "Lexicon: Strong's H1245—*baqash*," accessed January 9, 2020, https://www.blueletterbible.org/lang/lexicon/lexicon.cfm?Strongs=H1245&t=ESV.

9. Blue Letter Bible, "Lexicon: Strong's H7291—*radaph*, accessed January 9, 2020, https://www.blueletterbible.org/lang/lexicon/lexicon.cfm?Strongs=H7291&t=ESV.

10. Blue Letter Bible, "Lexicon: Strong's H8085—*shama'*," accessed November 24, 2019, https://www.blueletterbible.org/lang/lexicon/lexicon.cfm?Strongs=H8085&t=ESV.

WEEK 4: WITH OTHERS IN THE DARKNESS

1. Bible Hub, "Ahimelech," accessed January 8, 2020, https://biblehub.com/topical/a/ahimelech.htm.

2. Blue Letter Bible, "Matthew Henry: Commentary on 1 Samuel 21," accessed January 10, 2020, https://www.blueletterbible.org/Comm/mhc/1Sa/1Sa_021.cfm?a=257001 (italics in the original).

3. As an interesting note, in Mark 2:26, Jesus seems to indicate that David wasn't entirely alone. If you want to dig into this, I suggest using a study Bible, but definitely read it in the *The Message* version, too, as it's worded in an easy-to-understand way.

4. Lindsay Letters, https://lindsayletters.co/products/god-is-stronger?_pos=2&_sid =983b65d42&_ss=r.

5. Thomas Fulton and Kristen Poole, eds., *The Bible on the Shakespearean Stage: Cultures of Interpretation in Reformation England* (New York: Cambridge University Press, 2018), 116.

6. As we know, not every resource we find online is credible. So here are a few tips for turning up reliable facts: Google Books offers scans of many full books, and published resources have typically been through fact-checking. Sites like Wikipedia are less reliable, but if you check the cited sources at the bottom of a Wikipedia page, you'll find books and links that are more trustworthy. If you want to get a sense of how a biblical site looks today, you can find a variety of pictures on Google Images.

7. Bible Study Tools, "Adullam," accessed January 10, 2020, https://www.biblestudytools .com/dictionary/adullam/.

8. Gershon Galil and Moshe Weinfeld, eds., *Studies in Historical Geography and Biblical Historiography: Presented to Zecharia Kallai* (Leiden: Brill, 2000), 158.

9. Blue Letter Bible, "Lexicon: Strong's H123—*'Edom*," accessed November 26, 2019, https://www.blueletterbible.org/lang/lexicon/lexicon.cfm?Strongs=H123&t=ESV.

10. Blue Letter Bible, "Matthew Henry: Commentary on Psalms 52," accessed November 26, 2019, https://www.blueletterbible.org/comm/mhc/psa/psa_052.cfm.

11. Matthew Henry, *The Holy Bible: The Text According to the Authorized Version; and A Commentary* (London: The Religious Tract Society, 1836), 187.

12. Blue Letter Bible, "Charles Spurgeon: Commentary on Psalm 52," accessed February 10, 2020, https://www.blueletterbible.org/Comm/spurgeon_charles/tod/ps052.cfm?a=530008.

WEEK 5: TREASURES IN THE DARKNESS

1. *NIV Archaeological Study Bible: An Illustrated Walk through Biblical History and Culture* (Grand Rapids, MI: Zondervan, 2005), 608.
2. Not her real name.
3. Elizabeth Kübler-Ross, *Death: The Final Stage of Growth* (New York: Touchstone, 1976), 96.
4. Teresa Swanstrom Anderson, *Beautifully Interrupted: When God Holds the Pen That Writes Your Story* (Franklin, TN: Worthy Books, 2018), 223–238.
5. In one of her Bible study videos—I don't recall which one.
6. Blue Letter Bible, "Matthew Henry: Commentary on Psalms 63," accessed November 26, 2019, https://www.blueletterbible.org/Comm/mhc/Psa/Psa_063.cfm?a=541001.
7. As quoted in Rick Warren, *The Purpose Driven Life: What on Earth Am I Here For?* (Grand Rapids, MI: Zondervan, 2012), 197.
8. Bible Study Tools, *Smith's Bible Dictionary*, "Watches of the Night," accessed November 26, 2019, https://www.biblestudytools.com/dictionary/watches-of-night/.
9. Bible Study Tools, *Baker's Evangelical Dictionary of Biblical Theology*, "Hand, Right Hand," accessed November 26, 2019, https://www.biblestudytools.com/dictionaries/bakers-evangelical-dictionary/hand-right-hand.html.
10. Bible Study Tools, "Hand, Right Hand."

WEEK 6: STEPPING INTO DARKNESS

1. If you'd like to learn more about this fascinating book of the Bible, I recommend watching this brief but helpful video: The Bible Project, "Overview: 2 Samuel," March 26, 2016, https://www.youtube.com/watch?v=YvoWDXNDJgs.
2. Jeff Buckley, "Hallelujah," *Grace* © 1994 Columbia.
3. Shekinah Pastor's Pen, "When Kings Go to War," March 3, 2017, http://www.shekinahchurch.org/when-kings-go-to-war/.
4. Actually, according to one commentary, this was common practice: "The Hebrews . . . rose at daybreak, and always took a nap during the heat of the day. Afterwards they lounged in the cool of the evening on their flat-roofed terraces. It is probable that David had ascended to enjoy the open-air refreshment earlier than usual"; Blue Letter Bible, "Jamieson, Fausset & Brown: Commentary on 2 Samuel 11," accessed January 10, 2020, https://www.blueletterbible.org/Comm/jfb/2Sa/2Sa_011.cfm?a=278001.
5. Brené Brown, "Exhaustion Is Not a Status Symbol," interview by Lillian Cunningham, *Washington Post*, October 3, 2012, https://www.washingtonpost.com/national/exhaustion-is-not-a-status-symbol/2012/10/02/19d27aa8-0cba-11e2-bb5e-492c0d30bff6_story.html.
6. Carl Hagensick, "Nine Men in the Life of Bathsheba," heraldmag.org, accessed November 26, 2019, http://www.heraldmag.org/literature/bio_1.htm.
7. NOVA, "The Palace of King David," PBS, November 17, 2008, https://www.pbs.org/wgbh/nova/article/palace-king-david/.
8. Focus on the Family counseling line: 1-855-771-HELP (4357); Focus on the Family prayer line: 1-877-233-4455.

9. Blue Letter Bible, "Lexicon: Strong's G3875—*paraklētos*," accessed November 27, 2019, https://www.blueletterbible.org/lang/lexicon/lexicon.cfm?Strongs =G3875&t=ESV.

10. Bible Gateway, "John 14:16-17: The Passion Translation (TPT)," accessed November 27, 2019, https://www.biblegateway.com/passage/?search=John+14%3A16+&version =TPT.

11. *ESV Study Bible* (Wheaton, IL: Crossway, 2008), 1001.

WEEK 7: SAYING YES

1. "What Is the Difference Between the Words 'Tzur' and 'Selah' (Which Both Mean Rock)?" mí yodeya, accessed November 29, 2019, https://judaism.stackexchange .com/questions/30554/what-is-the-difference-between-the-words-tzur-and-selah -which-both-mean-roc.

2. Rabbi YY Jacobson, "Why Was Moses Denied the Promised Land?: I Am a Rock," TheYeshiva.net, accessed November 29, 2019, http://www.theyeshiva.net/jewish/960?beta=true&s=carticle.

3. Rabbi YY Jacobson, "Why Was Moses Denied?"

4. Mother Teresa, *In the Heart of the World: Thoughts, Stories and Prayers* (Novato, CA: New World Library, 2010), 19.

5. Blue Letter Bible, "Lexicon: Strong's H7121—*qara'*," accessed November 29, 2019, https://www.blueletterbible.org/lang/lexicon/lexicon.cfm?Strongs=H7121&t=ESV.

6. *ESV Study Bible*, 958.

7. Blue Letter Bible, "Matthew Henry: Commentary on Psalms 18," accessed November 29, 2019, https://www.blueletterbible.org/Comm/mhc/Psa/Psa_018.cfm?a=496017.

8. Blue Letter Bible, "Matthew Henry: Commentary on Psalms 18."

9. Blue Letter Bible, "C. H. Spurgeon: Psalm 18," accessed November 29, 2019, https:// www.blueletterbible.org/Comm/spurgeon_charles/tod/ps018.cfm?a=496017.

10. Blue Letter Bible, "C. H. Spurgeon: Psalm 18."

11. Blue Letter Bible, "Lexicon: Strong's H6588—*pesha'*," accessed November 29, 2019, https://www.blueletterbible.org/lang/lexicon/lexicon.cfm?Strongs=H6588&t=ESV.

12. Blue Letter Bible, "Lexicon: Strong's H2822—*choshek*," accessed December 1, 2019, https://www.blueletterbible.org/lang/lexicon/lexicon.cfm?Strongs=H2822&t=ESV.